WORLD CUP 82

The essential handbook for every football fan –
young and old – this summer.

Philip Evans has written articles, short stories
and books concerned with football, cares
especially about the fortunes of Barnsley and
Fiorentina, hopes that your particular favourite
team has good fortune and, above all, that this
edition of the World Cup produces some
exciting football.

D1369128

Acknowledgements

I would like to thank the following who have given me ideas or facts that have been used in this book: Manfred Haggan in West Germany, Dino Lanati and Roberto Cianfanelli in Italy, Robert Lipscomb in France, Lawrence Smith in Argentina, Chris Rhys for his great help, Brian Glanville of *The Sunday Times*, John Gill, Leslie Vernon, Ernest Hecht, Colin Malam and John Moynihan of the *Sunday Telegraph*, David Connolly, Jock Jardine, Ken Pritchard, Kieron Browne and Juliet Brightmore who helped to choose the photographs. Elizabeth Roy has been a wise and understanding editor.

Photograph credits

Page 1 Popperfoto/Keystone Press Agency Ltd; p. 2 Keystone Press Agency Ltd/Popperfoto; p. 3 Keystone Press Agency Ltd; p. 4 Keystone Press Agency Ltd/Popperfoto; p. 5 Popperfoto/Keystone Press Agency Ltd; p. 6 Popperfoto; p. 7 Popperfoto; p. 8 Keystone Press Agency Ltd/Popperfoto; p. 9 Syndication International Ltd/Popperfoto; pp. 10–15 Popperfoto; p. 16 Popperfoto/Keystone Press Agency Ltd.

WORLD CUP 82

Philip Evans

KNIGHT BOOKS
Hodder and Stoughton

For Matthew

Copyright © 1973/1982 Philip Evans

*This new edition first published by
Knight Books 1982*

British Library C.I.P.

Evans, Philip
  World Cup 82.—(Knight books)
  1. World cup (soccer)
  I. Title
  796.334'66   GV943.5 1982

ISBN 0 340 27747 5

Printed and bound in Great Britain for
Hodder and Stoughton Paperbacks, a
division of Hodder and Stoughton Ltd.,
Mill Road, Dunton Green, Sevenoaks,
Kent (Editorial Office: 47 Bedford
Square, London, WC1 3DP) by
Cox & Wyman Ltd, Reading

CONTENTS

PROLOGUE

This twelfth edition of the FIFA World Cup is larger than any that has gone before, so it comes as no surprise to learn that a record number of countries, 109, expressed interest before the qualifying rounds began to discover which 22 teams would join Argentina and Spain who qualify automatically as Champions and Hosts. This enlargement of the tournament has been given encouragement by the present President of FIFA, Joao Havelange of Brazil, 62 on 8 May, who succeeded Sir Stanley Rous on 11 June 1974 and who has always wanted wider participation in the tournament from countries of 'the Third World'.

The qualifying tournament was full of suspense up until the last moment, when the twenty-fourth qualifier, New Zealand, had to win a play-off match against China before a vehemently pro-China crowd in Singapore. The CONCACAF and African sections were full of last-minute tension. In the CONCACAF pool finals, held at Tegucigalpal's Estadoiol Nacional in the Honduras, both Canada and Mexico failed to force victories in their final matches against Cuba and Honduras respectively and so allowed El Salvador through by way of the back door. Morocco, managed by Just Fontaine, lost to Cameroon and Algeria was forced to beat Nigeria (in front of a vast and manic crowd in Lagos) to ease their way through.

The surprise in the South American section came in the 2–1 victory of Peru in Montevideo which led to the failure to qualify of Uruguay, the Champions of 1930 and 1950, and victors in the tournament held in Montevideo during the January of 1981 between all those teams who had won the World Cup. England chose not to compete, her place being taken by Holland, twice beaten finalists in the last two World Cups. But Holland was another team who failed to qualify for the 1982 World Cup, drawn as she was in a most difficult European Group along with Belgium, France (who both qualified) as well as with Eire, who took three points off her in the two games they played. In truth,

Eire was desperately unlucky not to qualify, being beaten on goal difference and having been forced to undergo some diabolical refereeing in both the matches against Belgium and in the game in Paris.

The only other team who failed to qualify on goal difference, Wales, omitted to take up the favour given to them by Czechoslovakia who could only manage a 1–1 draw in Iceland: a result which meant that Wales had to secure a nice victory against Iceland some three weeks later. This should have been very possible for the Welsh had won 4–0 when they themselves had played in Reykjavik but could do no better than scrape a 2–2 draw at home.

It was the European qualifying Group IV which provided the most erratic results, however, and helped the cause of England who had suffered 1–2 defeats in both Basle and Oslo against Switzerland and Norway. 'We now have to wait for someone to play worse than us,' remarked an embittered supporter of England on the morning after the second of those disasters. And so it happened with Switzerland taking three points off Rumania and handsomely easing England's path. England qualified while Holland, Eire and Wales did not – but sport has always had its injustices, as was seen in the most contrived (and fumbled!) decisions for the First Round Draw on January 16. The finals between mid-June and mid-July will see a total of 52 matches played in 29 days that will produce some good football, some refereeing decisions that will be argued over and a fair amount of tension off the field. Spanish football saw a major player, Quini, being kidnapped in March 1981; the security authorities will have been well-practised at using tanks, water-hose, tear-gas and all other forms of riot control; Basque terrorists may well use the event to press forward with their particular claims; and there is every possibility that the pressures, the immense prestige and wealth that ensue from victory in this tournament will mean that considerations other than sporting ones will rule supreme. The European Nations Championship of 1980 produced matches which were 'of no consequence' and totally lacked any spark of excitement. Let's hope for better things on this occasion.

1 A LOOK AT PREVIOUS TOURNAMENTS (1930-1958)

The idea of this book is to provide a readable and interesting guide to what we all may hope to see from what will be the twelfth World Cup Final tournament to be held in Spain in June and July. But before looking at some of the teams and players who may be taking part, let us look at the past tournaments.

One reason lies in the fascination with the past and the need to recognise that the great players of the past might have been truly great – whatever their date of birth! The other reason is entirely more prosaic: that of looking at power-balances. For instance, most people readily admit that the recent teams from Brazil and West Germany have had the players and methods to most excite coaches and spectators everywhere; and we must not leave out the Holland team of the past few years. But before the war Italy won the trophy twice; and throughout the history of the tournament there have been strong teams from both Europe and South America.

We might point out at the start that 'the World Cup' was something of a misnomer; that its proper name during the years for which it was competed was 'the Jules Rimet Trophy'. The principle of an international tournament was agreed in 1920 by FIFA – Federation of International Footballing Associations – and although it was ten years before the first tournament came to be played, the guiding light behind the idea, and the man who most worked to get the tournament going was Jules Rimet, President of the French Football Federation. Thus the attractive gold trophy – won outright in 1970 by the Brazil team – came to be given his name. And the new trophy, won for the first time in 1974 by West Germany, was entitled the 'FIFA World Cup'.

A sense of history might help us to remember why the achievement of British and Irish football has often been so mediocre – when seen in international terms. The fact is that by

1930 – the year of the first tournament – the four British countries had withdrawn their associations from FIFA and were thus
ineligible to compete. In 1938, it seemed the rule might be
waived and, indeed, England were invited to play the rôle of
guest team – once Austria had been overrun by the Nazis. But
the offer was refused, and it was not until the first post-war
tournament came to be played in Brazil in 1950, that any
British teams took part. Even on that occasion, the seeming
obstinacy and pig-headedness of the administrators had its way!
The British Home International Championships preceding the
Finals was recognised by FIFA as a qualifying group, in which the
first *two* teams could go to Brazil (in recent years the four home
countries have been very fortunate to get more than one place –
the only glaring exception being that of the 1958 Final tournament: when all *four* home countries qualified!) The Scots,
amazingly, decided that if they did not win the title – they would
not go to Brazil! The argument is one of those nonsensical ones
that ignores the large element of chance in sport – of whatever
kind. The Scots lost 1-0 to England at Hampden – and like
Achilles sulking in his tent, stayed at home to lick the communal
wound.

But this loss of twenty years – playing against the opposition
with the will to win – was something badly missed by the four
countries. If Britain gave modern football to the world then the
world soon caught up with, and overtook, us in terms of skill,
ball-control and tactics. Internationals played as 'friendlies'
were all very well but who can forget the way England players –
including Finney and Matthews – were received when they
returned from Brazil in 1950 – where they had ignominiously
been defeated by a team from the U.S.A.? And the lessons they
were shown three years later by the brilliant teams who came
from Hungary. Let alone the failure of England to qualify for
the Final tournaments of 1974 and 1978!

We have to face the fact that – as in many things – the pupil
has begun to outstrip the master; and forced him to get back to
basic principles himself. Sport – as most things – goes round in
cycles, and if it is any country's turn to get back and brush

up the basic techniques – those will stand them in good stead in
years to come.

World Cup 1930 – held in Uruguay

Not unnaturally the first tournament was a strange affair. Travel
to Uruguay from Europe at the time was costly and time-
consuming. Little wonder then that so many of the European
competitors withdrew – Italy, Spain, Austria, Hungary, Germany, Switzerland and Czechoslovakia among them. In many
ways one of the stars of the show proved to be King Carol of
Rumania – he not only picked the Rumanian team, but ensured
that the players were given adequate time off from their firms.
With only France, Belgium and Yugoslavia of the other European countries being involved, the affair was set for a South
American victory.

Why Uruguay as the place to hold a tournament such as this?
It seems strange; but the fact is that the Uruguayans had taken
the Olympic titles both in 1924 and 1928, they had promised to
build a handsome new stadium in which the games could be
played and had further guaranteed the expenses of all the
competing teams.

Thirteen countries competed in four pools, the winners of
each pool moving to the semi-final stage, together with the final
played on a knock-out basis.

When it came to it, two of the semi-finalists could be ranked as
surprises, one as a complete surprise. That was the United
States, for so long the chopping-block for skilful South American
teams in Olympic competition, but now able to use some formidable ex-British professionals. In their first game the Americans
tanned Belgium 3-0; then beat Paraguay by the same score and
qualified for the semi-finals where they would meet Argentina.

The Argentinians themselves had won their group without dropping a point, and the other semi-finalists were Yugoslavia – winners by 2-1 over Brazil and 4-0 over Bolivia; and the host team, Uruguay who scratched and scraped to find their form before going through against Peru 1-0 and then took the Rumanians to the cleaners by four goals to none. The stage was set for the South Americans to face the invaders.

In the event, the semi-finals were an anti-climax. Against a skilful and ruthless Argentinian team, the strength and brawn of the United States team proved ineffective – they went down by six goals to one. And in the other game, the Uruguayans thrashed Yugoslavia by the same score.

Both victorious teams were undoubtedly strong. The Uruguayans had prepared for the tournament with a dedication that has recently been commonplace, then considered extraordinary, one that made nonsense of any thought that they were still amateurs. For two celibate months the players had been trained ruthlessly, deprived of freedom, a rigorous curfew imposed on their nocturnal wanderings. When their brilliant goalkeeper, Mazzali, was discovered late one night, shoes in hand, sneaking in after a night on the town he was thrown out and his place given to a reserve.

There has never been much love lost between South American teams on the football field, and the natural rivalry that already existed between Uruguay and Argentina had recently been pointed by the defeat of the latter at the hands of the former in the final of the 1928 Olympic tournament.

The Final, strangely, was played in a comparatively peaceful way, the Uruguayans winning by four goals to two after having trailed by the odd goal in three at half-time. Off the field and after the game came the expected Argentinian protests – that the Uruguayans had been 'brutal', that the referee had been bought. Relations between the footballing authorities of the two countries were broken off. But the first World Cup had been played – and won handsomely by a very good team.

1930 – Final Stages

Semi-Finals

ARGENTINA 6, UNITED STATES 1 (1-0)

ARGENTINA: Botasso; Della Torre, Paternoster; Evaristo, J., Monti, Orlandini; Peucelle, Scopelli, Stabile, Ferreira (capt.), Evaristo, M.
USA: Douglas; Wood, Moorhouse; Gallacher, Tracey, Auld; Brown, Gonsalvez, Patenaude, Florie (capt.), McGhee.
SCORERS: Monti, Scopelli, Stabile (2), Peucelle (2) for Argentina; Brown for USA.

URUGUAY 6, YUGOSLAVIA 1 (3-1)

URUGUAY: Ballesteros; Nasazzi (capt.), Mascheroni; Andrade, Fernandez, Gestido; Dorado, Scarone, Anselmo, Cea, Iriarte.
YUGOSLAVIA: Yavocic; Ivkovic (capt.), Mihailovic; Arsenievic, Stefanovic, Djokic; Tirnanic, Marianovic, Beck, Vujadinovic, Seculic.
SCORERS: Cea (3), Anselmo (2), Iriarte for Uruguay; Seculic for Yugoslavia.

Final

URUGUAY 4, ARGENTINA 2 (1-2)

URUGUAY: Ballesteros; Nasazzi (capt.), Mascheroni; Andrade, Fernandez, Gestido; Dorado, Scarone, Castro, Cea, Iriarte.
ARGENTINA: Botasso; Della Torre, Paternoster; Evaristo, J., Monti, Suarez; Peucelle, Varallo, Stabile, Ferreira (capt.), Evaristo, M.
SCORERS: Dorado, Cea, Iriarte, Castro for Uruguay; Peucelle, Stabile for Argentina.

World Cup 1934 – held in Italy

Four years later, the competition was altogether more representative and better attended. The Uruguayans stayed away – piqued by the refusal of so many European teams to grace their tournament in 1930; and the Argentinians, having lost too many of their star players to Italian clubs, came with something of a reserve side. More important was the background to the tournament, played in Fascist Italy. Mussolini's features stared up from the official booklets, stared down from the Tribune of Honour in the various stadia.

In the event, the Italians had a fine team, pulled together by Vittorio Pozzo, a remarkable manager. It contained three Argentinians of supposed Italian extraction – the fearsome Monti among them. They were included on the justification that if they were eligible to do military service for Italy, they were eligible to play football for Italy. From the start Pozzo proved himself a master psychologist – and he needed to be. He was dealing with temperamental stars of great technical ability in individual terms, with little will to play with and for each other. Pozzo it was who welded together a squad of seeming disparates by locking the players up *in ritiro*, forcing them to live and train closely together, matching the prima donna antics of the one against those of the other, until all came to feel that they were being treated equally. Although the strong Austrian *wunderteam* was there, although Hungary and Spain could be fancied, many things pointed towards a second victory in the tournament for the team playing at 'home'.

In fact, there were several organisational changes from the first tournament. Whereas all the games in Uruguay had been played in the new stadium, purpose-built in Montevideo, it had been realised that in future more than one city would be needed to accommodate all the games. In Uruguay, thirteen teams had competed; here there were sixteen, this complete turnout allowing a change in the formula so that the tournament was a knock-out affair from first to last; and the cities that were graced by first-round ties were eight – Rome, Naples, Florence, Milan, Turin, Bologna, Genoa and Trieste.

The gallant Americans were there, ready to prove that their performance in 1930 had been no flash in the pan; but they met Italy in the first round and lost by seven goals to one. Spain, with the fabulous Zamora in goal, beat Brazil 3-1; the Germans, another team not to be under-valued, beat Belgium 5-2; Austria scraped through against France by the odd goal in five and after extra time; and Hungary revenged the bitter humiliation of having lost to Egypt in the 1924 Olympiad. On to the second round, with Italy and Spain drawn against each other.

Zamora was much feared, a goalkeeper who in the past had too often barred the way of Italian forwards not to be taken seriously, even at his current age of thirty-three. In the event he played a superb game, plucking centres and corner-kicks out of the air with sure timing and adhesive hands. But his courage had a price to be paid. Although he withstood 120 minutes of pressure as the game – stymied at 1-1 – moved into extra time, there seemed little chance at the final whistle that he would be fit to play the next day when the replay was due to take place.

Nor did he. And although the Spanish held Italy to just the one goal, they had been forced to field five other reserves. When played, the second game was even more pathetically refereed, so badly that the Swiss official concerned was suspended by his own federation. The Italians were through, but with that smear of luck that successful teams will always need to make their point.

To join them in the semi-finals came Germany – well organised in defence, and fortunate that the Swedes were down to ten men for much of their 2-1 victory; Austria, who beat Hungary by the same score in a brawling game that could never have suited the Austrians' penchant for swift, close passing; and Czechoslovakia, who came through against Switzerland 3-2.

That left Italy to face the fancied Austrians only two days after that bruising replay against Spain, and though there was only the one goal in their favour, their command was seldom in question. The Austrians were forced to wait until the forty-second minute before even aiming a shot at goal.

In the Final, the Italians came face to face with Czechoslovakia, much too clever for the Germans in the previous round, and were given a real run for their money. The Czechs took the lead through Puc in the middle of the second half, soon after missed two golden chances and hit a post. You shouldn't be allowed such freedom in competition, and much to their dismay the Czechs found Italy equalising with only eight minutes to go – a freak goal from Orsi, struck with his right foot and curling wickedly in the air. (The following day in practice, he tried twenty times – without success – to repeat it.) In the seventh minute of extra time, the Italians scored the winning goal through Schiavio and that was that – victory snatched from the enterprising Czechs just when they seemed to have the thing in the bag.

Neutral experts were eager to make their points. The advantage of home ground, they pointed out, had been decisive (it always is, surely); the frenzied, para-military support; the consequent intimidation of referees – these all may have been decisive. They may, but no one doubted that the 'World Cup' was now firmly established, on the road to improvement in terms of organisation and skill.

1934 – Final Stages

Semi-Finals

CZECHOSLOVAKIA 3, GERMANY 1 (1-0). *Rome*

CZECHOSLOVAKIA: Planika (capt.); Burger, Ctyroky; Kostalek, Cambal, Krcil; Junek, Svoboda, Sobotka, Nejedly, Puc.
GERMANY: Kress; Haringer, Busch; Zielinski, Szepan (capt.), Bender; Lehner, Siffling, Conen, Noack, Kobierski.
SCORERS: Nejedly (2), Krcil for Czechoslovakia; Noack for Germany.

ITALY 1, AUSTRIA 0 (1-0). *Milan*

ITALY: Combi (capt.); Monzeglio, Allemandi; Ferraris IV,
Monti, Bertolini; Guaita, Meazza, Schiavio, Ferrari, Orsi.
AUSTRIA: Platzer; Cisar, Sesztar; Wagner, Smistik (capt.),
Urbanek; Zischek, Bican, Sindelar, Schall, Viertel.
SCORER: Guaita for Italy.

Third Place Match

GERMANY 3, AUSTRIA 2 (3-1). *Naples*

GERMANY: Jakob; Janes, Busch; Zielinski, Muensenberg,
Bender; Lehner, Siffling, Conen, Szepan (capt.), Heidemann.
AUSTRIA: Platzer; Cisar, Sesztar; Wagner, Smistik (capt.),
Urbanek; Zischek, Braun, Bican, Horwath, Viertel.
SCORERS: Lehner (2), Conen for Germany; Horwath, Seszta for
Austria.

Final

ITALY 2, CZECHOSLOVAKIA 1 (0-0) (1-1) after extra time.
Rome

ITALY: Combi (capt.); Monzeglio, Allemandi; Ferraris IV,
Monti, Bertolini; Guiata, Meazza, Schiavio, Ferrari, Orsi.
CZECHOSLOVAKIA: Planika (capt.); Zenisek, Ctyroky; Kostalek,
Cambal, Krcil; Junek, Svoboda, Sobotka, Nejedly, Puc.
SCORERS: Orsi, Schiavio for Italy; Puc for Czechoslovakia.

World Cup 1938 – held in France

Again the tournament was played in several venues, again it was played along strictly knock-out lines, again it was won by Italy. And won more convincingly, it must be said. As if to prove that their football was the best in the world, the Italians had entered for, and won, the 1936 Olympiad – aided by the use of dubious 'amateurs', aided by the unpleasant Nazi ambience; but still a further victory to point to, further evidence that they had emerged as a powerful side.

Pozzo was still at the helm; to join Meazza in the forward line was Silvio Piola – a tall, powerful centre-forward who would score so many goals in Italian league football and for the international team; in place of the uncompromising Monti, Pozzo had at his disposal another South American hatchet-man in Andreolo of Uruguay; and to replace Combi in goal was yet another excellent keeper in Olivieri.

If victory in 1934 had been important to the Italians as a propaganda weapon, success in 1938 was deemed no less important and for the same reason. Political interest reared its head elsewhere. The Argentinians refused to come because they had not been given the competition; Spain was forced to withdraw on account of the bloody Civil War; and the Austrians – their country having been swallowed up by the Nazis – found themselves without a team for which to play. In fact, the 'German' team comprised seven players from Germany, four from Austria.

The first game went to 1-1; the replay panned out to a Swiss victory by four goals to two. Trailing by the odd goal in three into the second half, all seemed lost to the Swiss when they lost a player through injury. Not a bit of it. They waited for his return, equalised soon after, and then ran through for two more goals.

There were other surprises in store, given the context of history. The Dutch East Indies took part – annihilated by a formidable Hungarian side 6-0; and Cuba played well enough – beating the Rumanians after a replay in the first round – for

us to wonder what has happened to Cuban football in the last
three decades. Italy made heavy weather of Norway, winning by
the odd goal in three after extra time; and in an extraordinary
game, again needing extra time to decide the outcome, the Brazilians beat Poland 6-5. Playing at centre-forward for the South
Americans that day – and scorer, like the Pole, Willimowski, of
four goals – was Leonidas, the Black Diamond, a player of
extraordinary reflex and lightning anticipation. On to the second
round.

The Cubans came a great cropper at the hands of Sweden,
losing 8-0; the Hungarians, with the mercurial Sarosi at centre-
forward, put out gallant Switzerland 2-0; the Italians, their
morale revived by the cunning Pozzo, and thanks to two goals
from Piola, beat France 3-1; and the fireworks were reserved for
the game between the Brazilians and the Czechs.

It was nothing less than a holocaust, with three players – two
of them Brazilians – sent off, and two more retiring to hospital
with broken limbs. Not for nothing was the game to be known as
the 'Battle of Bordeaux', not for the last time was the tension of a
great occasion to prove too much for the Brazilians. They ran
out of spirit in the second half, after Leonidas had given them
the lead, gave away a penalty and the world rubbed its hands or
shielded its eyes in expectation of the replay.

In the event, the affair was peaceful, mild to an amazing
degree. The Brazilians made nine changes, the Czechs six;
Leonidas scored yet again, equalising the opening goal from the
Czechs, and Roberto it was who tucked away the winner.

And then came even more crazy an episode. Drawn against
the Italians, the Brazilian team manager announced that
Leonidas and Tim – his two great goal-scorers – would miss the
semi-final round and were being 'kept for the final'. Nobody
believed him, of course; but when the teams ran on to the pitch
– no Leonidas, no Tim. *Hamlet* without the Prince and Horatio
indeed; and playing straight into the hands of the Italians. They
scored the first two of the three goals in the game, were seldom
under hard pressure.

In the other semi-final Sweden scored a goal within the first

thirty-five seconds of play, then crumpled before the vaunted
Hungarian attack, who scored five times, thrice before half-
time. So dominant was the play of the central Europeans that for
much of the second half a large blackbird sat peacefully on the
field of play twenty yards away from the Hungarian goalkeeper.

Italy against Hungary in the Final, then; but first the play-
off for third place, and the salt really rubbed into Brazilian
wounds. Leonidas returned and scored two goals in a 4-2
victory over Sweden, posing questions that might have overtaxed
the Italian defence had he ever been given the chance to ask them
of it, and running out as the tournament's top scorer.

The Final itself seemed to be symbolised by the struggle
between two great centre-forwards; Piola for Italy, Sarosi for
Hungary. For all the skill of the latter, it was the bite and drive
of the former that proved decisive. Two early goals within a
minute provided a dramatic beginning; then the bustling style of
the Italians took them into a two-goal lead. Hungary came back
with twenty minutes to go through Sarosi, threatened briefly,
then went under finally with ten minutes to play when Piola
drove in the Italians' fourth goal.

Italy had unquestionably deserved her triumph this time. And
the World Cup would remain in Italian hands for twelve long
years while the world went to war and many players of talent
died violent deaths.

1938 – Final Stages

Semi-Finals

ITALY 2, BRAZIL 1 (2-0). *Marseilles*

ITALY: Olivieri; Foni, Rava; Serantoni, Andreolo, Locatelli;
Biavati, Meazza (capt.), Piola, Ferrari, Colaussi.
BRAZIL: Walter; Domingas Da Guia, Machados; Zeze, Martin
(capt.), Alfonsinho; Lopex, Luisinho, Peracio, Romeo, Patesko.
SCORERS: Colaussi, Meazza (penalty) for Italy; Romeo for Brazil.

HUNGARY 5, SWEDEN 1 (3-1). *Paris, Colombes*

HUNGARY: Szabo; Koranyi, Biro; Szalay, Turai, Lazar; Sas,
Szengeller, Sarosi (capt.), Toldi, Titkos.
SWEDEN: Abrahamson; Eriksson, Kjellgren; Almgren, Jacobsson,
Svanstroem; Wetterstroem, Keller (capt.), Andersson H.,
Jonasson, Nyberg.
SCORERS: Szengeller (3), Titkos, Sarosi for Hungary; Nyberg
for Sweden.

Third Place Match

BRAZIL 4, SWEDEN 2 (1-2). *Bordeaux*

BRAZIL: Batatoes; Domingas Da Guia, Machados; Zeze,
Brandao, Alfonsinho; Roberto, Romeo, Leonidas (capt.),
Peracio, Patesko.
SWEDEN: Abrahamson; Eriksson, Nilssen; Almgren, Linderholm,
Svanstroem (capt.); Berssen, Andersson H., Jonasson, Andersson, A., Nyberg.
SCORERS: Jonasson, Nyberg for Sweden; Romeo, Leonidas (2),
Peracio for Brazil.

Final

ITALY 4, HUNGARY 2 (3-1). *Paris, Colombes*

ITALY: Olivieri; Foni, Rava; Serantoni, Andreolo, Locatelli;
Biavati, Meazza (capt.), Piola, Ferrari, Colaussi.
HUNGARY: Szabo; Polgar, Biro; Szalay, Szucs, Lazar; Sas,
Vincze, Sarosi (capt.), Szengeller, Titkos.
SCORERS: Colaussi (2), Piola (2) for Italy; Titkos, Sarosi for
Hungary.

World Cup 1950 – held in Brazil

Twenty years had elapsed since the tournament was last held
in South America, and the problems thrown up had not, it
appeared, been diluted. Thirteen teams had competed in 1930,
the tally in 1950 would be no larger. The Indians qualified, but
would not come; Scotland, as we have seen, fatuously stayed out;
the Austrians were going through one of their frequent bouts of
diffidence, and felt their team not strong enough (even though
they had just beaten Italy – who would play); Hungary, like
the Russians, remained in Cold War isolation; the French,
knocked out in their qualifying group, and then reprieved, felt
the journey too long and arduous; and the Argentinians had
squabbled with the Brazilian Federation. As for West Germany,
they were still barred from FIFA.

Thirteen teams, then; and the gaps made nonsense of the new
pool system, which would apply not merely to the four qualifying
groups, but also to the final group – competed in by the four
winners. The Uruguayans, for example, had only to play one
jog-trot of a game to be through to the final pool – a victory by
eight goals to none over Bolivia. Little wonder that they seemed
more fresh and zestful in the late stages of the tournament.

The massive Maracana stadium in Rio de Janeiro was still
being built when the tournament started – and when it finished.
Brazil featured there in the opening match, beating Mexico by
four clear goals in front of a happily partisan crowd of 155,000
(the Maracana would hold 200,000). Two of their goals came
from Ademir – yet another of those incredible ball-playing
inside forwards that the Brazilians had a penchant for producing.
Like the Uruguayans in 1930, the Italians in 1934, the Brazilians
had prepared with military thoroughness – an air of celibacy and
special diets reigned supreme. They would qualify for the final
pool – but not before drawing against Switzerland with a mis-
chosen team, and having to fight hard against a Yugoslavian side.

Co-favourites with Brazil were – England! Appearing for the
first time in the competition, with some devastating form behind

them, the English had to be fancied. Whatever the balance of power suggested, eyes turned interestedly towards them. They had yet to find a centre-forward to replace Lawton, but Matthews was there, Finney was there, Mortensen was there, Mannion was there; and these were players whose skill was legendary. They scraped through their first game against Chile, finding the heat and humidity so oppressive that they took oxygen at half-time. And then came the shock of the tournament – possibly one of the greatest shocks in the history of international football – as England went down by just the one goal to the United States.

A number of the American players had stayed up into the early hours of the morning; several of them expected a cricket score, and indicated as much to British journalists. In the event, it was eight minutes before half-time when Gaetjens headed in Bahr's cross (or was it a miskicked shot?); and that, whatever the English forwards would do in the second half, remained the only goal of the match. The victory of Chile over the Americans a few days later and by five goals to two emphasised England's shame. And although Matthews and Milburn were brought in for the final English game against Spain, although many felt the English deserved at least a draw, the die was cast. England were out of a tournament whose previous editions they had ignored, one for which they had been heavily favoured.

Into the final pool along with Spain, Brazil and Uruguay went Sweden. They had won the 1948 Olympic tournament with a team that included Gren, Nordhal and Liedholm – all, alas, now playing in Italy and blocked from selection. What irony, then, that in their first game the Swedes should play the Italians and win by the odd goal in five! A draw against the other team in their pool, Paraguay, and Sweden were through.

Little good it was to do them, with Brazil now turning on all the fireworks. In their first game the Brazilians beat Sweden 7-1; in their second, Spain by 6-1. Their trio of inside forwards – Jair, Ademir and Zizinho – seemed uncontrollable: professional counterparts of those countless boys who juggle footballs on the Copacabana beach from sunrise to sunset. Brazil, it seemed, would handsomely win the title.

The challenge came from Uruguay, held to a draw by Spain, victors over Sweden (who would in turn defeat the Spanish with that perverse logic that accompanies these affairs). If the Brazilians had Jair, Ademir and Zizinho – the Uruguayans had Juan Schiaffino, as thin as a piece of paper, a player of enormous technical skills that would later be appreciated by European audiences when he found his way into the cauldron of Italian league football, once described by Tommy Docherty as the best player he ever had to face.

But for all Schiaffino's skills, the Uruguayans were the first to admit that they were unable to match the Brazilians in terms of pure technique. Tactical expertise was needed, and tactical expertise was used. Hard as they might try, the Brazilian forwards seldom seemed able to penetrate the light-blue defensive barrier thrown up by the Uruguayan defence, the dark mastery of Maspoli in the opposing goal. No score at half-time.

Two minutes after the interval, the Maracana erupted as Friaça closed in from the wing, shot – and scored. But the Uruguayans had made their point, knew that they were able to cope with the 'superteam' that opposed them. Schiaffino it was who put them ahead, ghosting through the centre to knock in a cross. And ten minutes before the end, Ghiggia, the Uruguayan left-wing, cut in, beat his fullback to score.

The 'right team' had lost; Uruguay had won a match of breath-taking quality and the tournament for a second time after an interval of twenty years.

1950 – Final Stages

Final Pool

URUGUAY 2, SPAIN 2 (1-2). *São Paulo*

URUGUAY: Maspoli; Gonzales, M., Tejera; Gonzales, W., Varela (capt.), Andrade; Ghiggia, Perez, Miguez, Schiaffino, Vidal.
SPAIN: Ramallets; Alonzo, Gonzalvo II; Gonzalvo III, Parra, Puchades; Basora, Igoa, Zarra, Molowny, Gainza.
SCORERS: Ghiggia, Varela for Uruguay; Basora (2) for Spain.

BRAZIL 7, SWEDEN 1 (3-1). *Rio*

BRAZIL: Barbosa; Augusto (capt.), Juvenal; Bauer, Danilo, Bigode; Maneca, Zizinho, Ademir, Jair, Chico.
SWEDEN: Svensson; Samuelsson, Nilsson, E.; Andersson, Nordahl, K., Gard; Sundqvist, Palmer, Jeppson, Skoglund, Nilsson, S.
SCORERS: Ademir (4), Chico (2), Maneca for Brazil; Andersson (penalty) for Sweden.

URUGUAY 3, SWEDEN 2 (1-2). *São Paulo*

URUGUAY: Paz; Gonzales, M., Tejera; Gambetta, Varela (capt.), Andrade; Ghiggia, Perez, Miguez, Schiaffino, Vidal.
SWEDEN: Svensson; Samuelsson, Nilsson, E.; Andersson, Johansson, Gard; Johnsson, Palmer, Melberg, Skoglund, Sundqvist.
SCORERS: Palmer, Sundqvist for Sweden; Ghiggia, Miguez (2) for Uruguay.

BRAZIL 6, SPAIN 1 (3-0). *Rio*

BRAZIL: Barbosa; Augusto (capt.), Juvenal; Bauer, Danilo, Bigode; Friaça, Zizinho, Ademir, Jair, Chico.

SPAIN: Eizaguirre; Alonzo, Gonzalvo II; Gonzalvo III, Parra, Puchades; Basora, Igoa, Zarra, Panizo, Gainza.
SCORERS: Jair (2), Chico (2), Zizinho, Parra (own goal) for Brazil; Igoa for Spain.

SWEDEN 3, SPAIN 1 (2-0). *São Paulo*

SWEDEN: Svensson; Samuelsson, Nilsson, E.; Andersson, Johansson, Gard; Sundqvist, Mellberg, Rydell, Palmer, Johnsson.
SPAIN: Eizaguirre; Asensi, Alonzo; Silva, Parra, Puchades; Basora, Fernandez, Zarra, Panizo, Juncosa.
SCORERS: Johansson, Mellberg, Palmer for Sweden; Zarra for Spain.

URUGUAY 2, BRAZIL 1 (0-0). *Rio*

URUGUAY: Maspoli; Gonzales, M., Tejera; Gambetta, Varela (capt.), Andrade; Ghiggia, Perez, Miguez, Schiaffino, Moran.
BRAZIL: Barbosa; Augusto (capt.), Juvenal; Bauer, Danilo, Bigode; Friaça, Zizinho, Ademir, Jair, Chico.
SCORERS: Friaça for Brazil; Schiaffino, Ghiggia for Uruguay.

Final Positions

					Goals		
	P	W	D	L	F	A	Pts
Uruguay	3	2	1	0	7	5	5
Brazil	3	2	0	1	14	4	4
Sweden	3	1	0	2	6	11	2
Spain	3	0	1	2	4	11	1

World Cup 1954 – held in Switzerland

And here was another instance of the 'wrong' team coming through to take the trophy, when Germany won their first World Cup and the brilliant Hungarians were denied their right. Bizarre organisation in which two teams from each group were 'seeded', leaving the supposedly stronger teams apart in the early stages; and the presence of a handful of really formidable teams in Hungary, Brazil, Germany, Uruguay and Austria – both these ensured that in later years this would come to be known as the last of the 'open' tournaments, the last in which teams seemed more concerned to score, than to prevent, goals.

England were there, shaky after a hammering administered at the hands of the Hungarians only a couple of weeks earlier when their winter defeat at Wembley had been exposed as no fluke. In Budapest they lost 7-1, a disorganised rabble in front of brilliant passing and shooting. History was on their side, Matthews, Wright and Finney in it; but few gave them any chance. And Scotland were also there – having repeated one part of their rôle from 1950 by losing to England; this time, however, having the courage to enter in spite of their lack of confidence.

Uruguay were strong, entering their first European tournament, unbeaten to date. Schiaffino was still there; they had splendid new wingers in Abbadie and Borges; a powerful stopper in Santamaria, later to be the bulwark of Real Madrid's invincible side. The Brazilians were slightly fancied despite being involved in a period of neurotic assessment. Their game, they felt, was too ingenious; so they closed the defence with care, came down hard on flair unless it could be harnessed to teamwork. They would wait until 1958 before perfecting the balance, but in their first game of the tournament – a 5-0 drubbing of Mexico – they introduced two great backs in the Santoses (no relation), a fine distributor in Didì, a unique winger in Julinho –

a man of violent pace, superb balance, close control and with a
rocket of a shot.

In *their* first game, the Uruguayans beat the Czechs 2-0; then
annihilated Scotland by seven clear goals, Borges and Abbadie
getting five between them. The Scottish campaign had not been
helped by dissension off the pitch and the resignation, after the
first defeat at the hands of Austria, of Andy Beattie, the team
manager; but the Uruguayans looked good, Schiaffino in regal
form. Through to join them in the quarter-finals went Yugoslavia – who had held Brazil to a 1-1 draw in a memorable
match in which their goalkeeper Beara (a former ballet dancer)
had performed prodigies in defence and Zebec had given
evidence of his all-round skill; England, drawing 4-4 with
Belgium first time out before beating Switzerland 2-0; the Swiss,
thanks to a played-off game against the Italians, who had been
strangely static; Brazil; Austria, who defeated the Czechs 5-0
with their talented half-back Ocwirk emerging as one of the
players of the tournament; Germany and Hungary.

This last pair provided most of the news. The Hungarians
went out in their first game, drubbed Korea 9-0; then were
forced to play the Germans, the latter not having been seeded.
The wily German coach, Sepp Herberger, cleverly decided to
throw away this match, banked on winning the play-off against
Turkey (which he did) and fielded a team largely composed of
reserves. The Hungarians came through 8-3, the Germans had
not given away any secrets; but most important, it was in this
game that Puskas was injured, that a vital part of the Hungarian
machine was put out of action.

The Hungarians had won the 1952 Olympiad; in Hidegkuti
they had a deep-lying centre-forward of great verve and
authority, a man who could make and score brilliant goals; at
inside forward they had Kocsis and Puskas, the former a little
man with the neck of a bull who could leap great heights to head
a ball, the latter with a hammer of a left foot; and in the half-
back line they had an excellent exemplar in Boszik, always
driving forward with speed, ingenuity and strength. With four
players of genius and others who were little behind, it was easy

to see why the Hungarians were widely considered favourites to win the tournament.

Two things upset them. First, the injury to Puskas, who would play again only in the Final and at half-speed. The other was what came to be known as the 'Battle of Berne', a disgraceful quarter-final tie which pitted them against the Brazilians. Hungary won the game 4-2 after being two up in the first eight minutes, after giving away a penalty, after themselves scoring from one, after Nilton Santos and Boszik had been sent off for fighting in a match that seemed more suited to a boxing ring. After the game the Brazilians invaded the Hungarian dressing-room, went berserk and came close to inflicting further serious injury on the Hungarian players. Hungary were through to the semi-finals where they would play an unforgettable game against Uruguay, victors over an England team that fought hard, laid siege to the Uruguayan goal without really capitalising on their approach play (where Matthews was outstanding) and was let down by Merrick, the goalkeeper.

The other semi-final would be between Austria who beat Switzerland 7-5 after having trailed 2-4 at half-time; and Germany, ploughing on with force and thoroughness against the talented Yugoslavs. In the event, the Germans 'came good' when it mattered. They scored twice from penalties in their 6-1 win, now seemed ominously hard to beat.

The Hungary–Uruguay game, even without Puskas, was a gem. Two-nil up with fifteen minutes to go, the Hungarians seemed through – until the Uruguayans counter-attacked. Schiaffino put Hohberg through, the move was repeated three minutes before the end, and extra time was on. It nearly began without Hohberg himself, who had been forced to retire 'injured' after having been overwhelmed by delighted team mates. But recover he did, to burst through early in the first period of extra time and smack in a shot – that came back off a post. In retrospect, it can be seen as the turning point; for Kocsis twice in the second period rose to head home crosses; and Hungary were through.

A Puskas far from fit, too chubby round the middle and with a

sore ankle, returned for the Final. Great player though he was,
the Hungarians had managed well without him, and might have
done better to discard him (as Alf Ramsey would prefer Roger
Hunt to Jimmy Greaves twelve years later, sacrificing rare gifts
to teamwork, and win). Yet again, the Hungarians went off like a
train, two goals up in eight minutes, seemingly well on the way
to a victory that awaited them.

What mattered most, perhaps, was the swiftness of the German
reply. Three minutes later they had drawn back a goal through
Morlock; then Rahn drove home a corner; at the other end
Turek remained in stupendous form between the goalposts;
Rahn got the goal that would be the winner; Puskas scored –
only to be given offside; and the invincible Hungarians had
been beaten.

They had been beaten by a better team on the day; by the
punishment of earlier games against South Americans; by a
certain amount of internal dissension to do with the injury to
Puskas. Yet they remained the best team that Europe had seen to
date, possibly the best team that Europe has yet seen. And it
took an almost equally brilliant team from the other side of the
world and four years later, to push them into the light shadows;
the amazing Brazilians of the Sweden tournament, and their
latest wonder-boy – Pelé.

1954 – Final Stages

Quarter-Finals

GERMANY 2, YUGOSLAVIA 0 (1-0). *Geneva*

GERMANY: Turek; Laband, Kohlmeyer; Eckel, Liebrich, Mai;
Rahn, Morlock, Walter, O., Walter, F. (capt.), Schaefer.
YUGOSLAVIA: Beara; Stankovic, Crnkovic; Cjaicowski I, Horvat,
Boskov; Milutinovic, Mitic (capt.), Vukas, Bobek, Zebec.
SCORERS: Horvat (own goal), Rahn for Germany.

HUNGARY 4, BRAZIL 2 (2-1). *Berne*

HUNGARY: Grosics; Buzansky, Lantos; Boszik (capt.), Lorant,
Zakarias; Toth, M., Kocsis, Hidegkuti, Czibor, Toth, J.
BRAZIL: Castilho; Santos, D., Santos, N.; Brandaozinho,
Pinheiro (capt.), Bauer; Julinho, Didì, Indio, Tozzi, Maurinho.
SCORERS: Hidegkuti (2), Kocsis, Lantos (penalty) for Hungary;
Santos, D. (penalty), Julinho for Brazil.

AUSTRIA 7, SWITZERLAND 5 (2-4). *Lausanne*

AUSTRIA: Schmied; Hanappi, Barschandt; Ocwirk (capt.),
Happel, Koller; Koerner, R., Wagner, Stojaspal, Probst,
Koerner, A.
SWITZERLAND: Parlier; Neury, Kernen; Eggimann, Bocquet
(capt.), Casali; Antenen, Vonlanthen, Hugi, Ballaman, Fatton.
SCORERS: Ballaman (2), Hugi (2), Hanappi (own goal) for
Switzerland; Koerner, A. (2), Ocwirk, Wagner (3), Probst for
Austria.

URUGUAY 4, ENGLAND 2 (2-1). *Basel*

URUGUAY: Maspoli; Santamaria, Martinez; Andrade, Varela
(capt.), Cruz; Abbadie, Ambrois, Miguez, Schiaffino, Borges.
ENGLAND: Merrick; Staniforth, Byrne; McGarry, Wright (capt.),
Dickinson; Matthews, Broadis, Lofthouse, Wilshaw, Finney.
SCORERS: Borges, Varela, Schiaffino, Ambrois for Uruguay;
Lofthouse, Finney for England.

Semi-Finals

GERMANY 6, AUSTRIA 1 (1-0). *Basel*

GERMANY: Turek; Posipal, Kohlmeyer; Eckel, Liebrich, Mai;
Rahn, Morlock, Walter, O., Walter, F. (capt.), Schaefer.
AUSTRIA: Zeman; Hanappi, Schleger; Ocwirk (capt.), Happel,
Koller; Koerner, R., Wagner, Stojaspal, Probst, Koerner, A.

SCORERS: Schaefer, Morlock, Walter, F. (2 penalties), Walter, O. (2) for Germany; Probst for Austria.

HUNGARY 4, URUGUAY 2 (1-0) (2-2) after extra time. *Lausanne*

HUNGARY: Grosics; Buzansky, Lantos; Bostik (capt.), Lorant, Zakarias; Budai, Kocsis, Palotas, Hidegkuti, Czibor.
URUGUAY: Maspoli; Santamaria, Martinez; Andrade (capt.), Carballo, Cruz; Souto, Ambrois, Schiaffino, Hohberg, Borges.
SCORERS: Czibor, Hidegkuti, Kocsis (2) for Hungary; Hohberg (2) for Uruguay.

Third Place Match

AUSTRIA 3, URUGUAY 1 (1-1). *Zurich*

AUSTRIA: Schmied; Hanappi, Barschandt; Ocwirk (capt.), Kollman, Koller; Koener, R., Wagner, Dienst, Stojaspal, Probst.
URUGUAY: Maspoli; Santamaria, Martinez; Andrade (capt.), Carballo, Cruz; Abbadie, Hohberg, Mendez, Schiaffino, Borges.
SCORERS: Stojaspal (penalty), Cruz (own goal), Ocwirk for Austria; Hohberg for Uruguay.

Final

GERMANY 3, HUNGARY 2 (2-2). *Berne*

GERMANY: Turek; Posipal, Kohlmeyer; Eckel, Liebrich, Mai; Rahn, Morlock, Walter, O., Walter, F. (capt.), Schaefer.
HUNGARY: Grosics; Buzansky, Lantos; Boszik, Lorant (capt.), Zakarias; Czibor, Kocsis, Hidegkuti, Puskas, Toth, J.
SCORERS: Puskas, Czibor for Hungary; Morlock, Rahn (2) for Germany.

World Cup 1958 – held in Sweden

The Brazilians came and conquered – came to Sweden as one
of the favourites (thanks to the on-paper banality of much of the
opposition), conquered with an extraordinary demonstration of
prowess and skill in the Final. The backstage people concerned,
for the first time, harnessed the natural talent of the players,
made the team's play really effective. In 1950 the players had
been allowed to express themselves too freely; in 1954, they had
been too restrained. Now the blend was right.

Yet the truth remains, that like the Hungarians before them
but to a lesser degree, the Brazilians proved that great teams –
so called – depend essentially upon the coming-together in one
period of time of a clutch of great players. Didì was in evidence
again, full of lithe passes, famous for his 'falling leaf' shot –
struck with the outside of the foot and fading distressingly in
mid-flight; the Santoses were playing still at fullback; and in the
forward line were two new geniuses in Garrincha and the new
black prodigy, Pelé. And there was Zagalo, a player who covered
vast tracts of ground at electric pace, one with lungs of leather
and an astute footballing brain. The components were there, and
the world waited to see whether they could be put together.

All four British teams competed; the Welsh and Irish for the
first and – to date – last time. The former had a fine goalkeeper
in Kelsey, the majestic John Charles, a clever inside-forward in
Allchurch, an impish winger in Cliff Jones. The latter had
Danny Blanchflower and Jimmy McIlroy, but the Munich
air disaster had deprived them of Blanchflower's brother, Jackie,
a commanding centre-back. Both teams thrived on the intimate
atmosphere they created off the field, devoid of the paranoia
and bitching that had surrounded English team selection.

To be fair to England, they had suffered terribly from
Munich. The accident deprived them of Duncan Edwards, their
brilliant left-half; Tommy Taylor, a dangerous centre-forward;
and Roger Byrne, a resourceful back. Players such as these
could not be replaced overnight, admittedly; but some of the

selection was bizarre in the extreme. Lofthouse was left at home, when his experience might have been invaluable; and Bobby Charlton, whose amazing swerve and lethal shooting had delighted everyone in the previous three months, was taken – only to be left on the touchlines for the whole tournament. Courage, it seemed, was lacking – the courage that often wins matches and tournaments.

The Scots had eliminated Spain but lost 4-0 to England in Glasgow. Few held out for them much hope of success. The Hungarians had lost too many of their star players in the aftermath of the 1956 Revolution, and such as remained were long in the tooth. Argentina competed, but without its much-famed 'Trio of Death' in the inside forward positions – Maschio, Angelillo and Sivori – all playing with Italian clubs and ignored. And the Germans seemed weak, despite the continued and cunning presence of Herberger, the coach.

The Russians competed for the first time, having won the 1956 Olympiad in Australia. They had the amazing Yachin in goal, kept themselves to themselves, and would play the sturdy sort of game that one has come to expect from them in recent years – functionalism with just the occasional flash of forward and midfield genius.

Playing at home, the Swedes called upon several of their stars based in Italy – the elegant Liedholm, tall and commanding in midfield; Nacka Skoglund, a hero of their 1950 World Cup team; Gustavsson, a commanding centre-back; and Kurt Hamrin, an electric little outside-right. To begin with, their supporters were pessimistic, but pessimism soon changed to optimism.

No one anticipated much from the French, yet they were to be the revelation of the tournament. In their first game, they walked through Paraguay 7-3, three of the goals coming from Juste Fontaine, who had come to the tournament not expecting to gain a place. He would score thirteen goals in all – a record that will not easily be beaten. And alongside Fontaine was Kopa – small, strong, beautifully-balanced with fine control and the ability to give a defence-splitting pass.

Group IV was the focal point – Brazil, Russia, England and
Austria. The Brazilians beat the other two, drew a goalless game
against England, who also drew with Russia and Austria. To a
play-off, and the Russians came through by the one goal. If
only Tom Finney had not been injured in the first game of the
tournament. If only.

The Irish drew against the Germans, beat the Czechs, lost to
Argentina – who finished bottom of the pool! They came through
after a play-off against Czechoslovakia, by the odd goal in three,
with McParland scoring his second goal of the game in the first
period of extra time. Courage, in their case, had paid off.

The Scots drew with Yugoslavia, went down to both France
and Paraguay. Better news from the Welsh, who went to a
play-off in their pool against the Hungarians – and won 2-1
after trailing at half-time. The victory would put them through
against Brazil, and few gave them much hope.

That especially after the 'real' Brazil had played for the first
time in the third game of their qualifying group. Out had gone
Jose Altafini, nicknamed 'Mazzola' for his resemblance to the
great post-war Italian inside forward; a man who would play for
Italy in the 1962 finals, who at the age of thirty-four would
score against Derby County in the semi-final of the 1972–73
European Cup trophy goals that were *par excellence*, those of a
venomous striker. And in would come Garrincha and Pelé.

Both were to have an extraordinary effect on the 1958 competition, an extraordinary effect on players and spectators
throughout the world. Garrincha and Pelé – two of the great
instinctive players of the age, of any age. The former was a
winger who had all the powers of Matthews – the vicious swerve
that took him outside the full back, the ability to accelerate into
astonishing speed from a standing start. Despite – perhaps
because of – a curiously twisted knee, a legacy from birth, his
ball-control was exceptional. And Pelé, at seventeen, his head
pointed like a coconut, with all his legendary skills already
there for all to see – the ability to 'kill' a ball on thigh or chest,
to shoot ferociously from impossible angles, to head a ball with a
power that reminded people of Lawton or Kocsis.

So what chance Wales, against players such as these? In the event, much. If only John Charles had been fit to play, the one Welshman who could have put pressure on the Brazilian defence. As it was, the Welsh defence played superbly; and Pelé was later to describe the one goal of the match as the most important he had ever scored. And there's over a thousand to choose from!

Into the semi-finals with Brazil went France, Germany, Sweden. The Germans churned on, their ageing team and cunning management able to find answers to all the questions posed by the Yugoslavs. Sweden went through with Hamrin on venomous form – stockings rolled down, small and compact, hard to stop once he began to find his stride, scorer of the first goal against the Russians, maker of the second.

And there was France – the team no one was prepared to take seriously, even though they had won their qualifying group and scored eleven goals in the process. Against the Irish, Fontaine scored twice more to re-emphasise his effectiveness. Tired and depleted by injuries, the Irish had no cause for complaint. Their effort, like that of the Welsh, had been brave and dignified.

In the semi-finals, it was the turn of the French to suffer at the hands of Brazil. The score was still 1-1 when Jonquet, the elegant French centre-half was forced to retire in the thirty-seventh minute: a retirement that was to prove fatal as Pelé scored a hat trick and Brazil ran out winners 5-2. France would have consolation later, when they would defeat Germany in the match to decide third place by six goals to three, four coming from the incessant Fontaine.

Germany had proved no match for Sweden. The raucousness of German chanting at international matches is legendary, but in Sweden the German supporters found their match. As the Swedes progressed from round to round, so grew the noise of their fans, nationalist to the extreme. And so on the field, the Germans could find no answers to the wiles of Liedholm in midfield, the venom of Hamrin as he cut in from the wing. They would unearth a potentially great defender in Schnellinger, a powerful midfield player in Szymaniak – but the Germans knew that they deserved to be out.

In the Final, the Swedish crowd was silenced by FIFA. An
official had attended the semi-final game, put a stop to organised
cheering . . . and a Swedish crowd deprived of its cheerleaders
would scarcely cheer at all. Just the once, as Liedholm put
Sweden ahead after four minutes. 'When the Brazilians are a goal
down,' had said George Raynor, Sweden's Yorkshire coach,
'they panic all over the show.' But Raynor must have been
thinking of the overtrained 1954 Brazilians or the dazzling
unpredictables of 1950.

Twice, it was Garrincha; twice he swerved maniacally past
Swedish defenders and centred; twice Vavà rushed in to score.
And ten minutes after half-time it was Pelé's turn. Trapping a
long centre on his thigh, he hooked it over his head, slashed it
into the net. He would score Brazil's fifth goal with his head after
Zagalo had torn through for the fourth. And though Sweden
would get a second goal, that would be that.

The crowd applauded as the Brazilians did two laps of honour,
first with their own flag, then with that of the Swedes. Their
supporters chanted '*samba, samba*'. And the world knew that it
had seen a new style of football.

1958 – Final Stages

Quarter-Finals

FRANCE 4, IRELAND 0 (1-0) *Norrkoping*

FRANCE: Abbes; Kaelbel, Lerond; Penverne, Jonquet, Marcel;
Wisnieski, Fontaine, Kopa, Piantoni, Vincent.
IRELAND: Gregg; Keith, McMichael; Blanchflower, Cunning-
ham, Cush; Bingham, Casey, Scott, McIlroy, McParland.
SCORERS: Wisnieski, Fontaine (2), Piantoni for France.

GERMANY 1, YUGOSLAVIA 0 (1-0). *Malmo*

GERMANY: Herkenrath; Stollenwerk, Juskowiak; Eckel, Erhardt,
Szymaniak; Rahn, Walter, Seeler, Schmidt, Schaefer.
YUGOSLAVIA: Krivocuka; Sijakovic, Crnkovic; Krstic, Zebec,
Boskov; Petakovik, Veselinovic, Milutinovic, Ognjanovic,
Rajkov.
SCORER: Rahn for Germany.

SWEDEN 2, RUSSIA 0 (0-0). *Stockholm*

SWEDEN: Svensson; Bergmark, Axbom; Boerjesson, Gustavsson,
Parling; Hamrin, Gren, Simonsson, Liedholm, Skoglung.
RUSSIA: Yachin; Kessarev, Kuznetsov; Voinov, Krijevski,
Tsarev; Ivanov, A., Ivanov, V., Simonian, Salnikov, Ilyin.
SCORERS: Hamrin, Simonsson for Sweden.

BRAZIL 1 WALES 0 (0-0). *Gothenburg*

BRAZIL: Gilmar; De Sordi, Santos, N.; Zito, Bellini, Orlando;
Garrincha, Didì, Mazzola, Pelé, Zagalo.
WALES: Kelsey; Williams, Hopkins; Sullivan, Charles, M.,
Bowen; Medwin, Hewitt, Webster, Allchurch, Jones.
SCORER: Pelé for Brazil.

Semi-Finals

BRAZIL 5, FRANCE 2 (2-1). *Stockholm*

BRAZIL: Gilmar; De Sordi, Santos, N.; Zito, Bellini, Orlando;
Garrincha, Didì, Vavà, Pelé, Zagalo.
FRANCE: Abbes; Kaelbel, Lerond; Penverne, Jonquet, Marcel;
Wisnieski, Fontaine, Kopa, Piantoni, Vincent.
SCORERS: Vavà, Didì, Pelé (3) for Brazil; Fontaine, Piantoni for
France.

SWEDEN 3, GERMANY 1 (1-1). *Gothenberg*

SWEDEN: Svensson; Bergmark, Axbom; Boerjesson, Gustavsson,
Parling; Hamrin, Gren, Simonsson, Liedholm, Skoglund.
GERMANY: Herkenrath; Stollenwerk, Juskowiak; Eckel, Erhardt,
Szymaniak; Rahn, Walter, Seeler, Schaefer, Cieslarczyk.
SCORERS: Schaefer for Germany; Skoglund, Gren, Hamrin for
Sweden.

Third Place Match

FRANCE 6, GERMANY 3 (0-0). *Gothenburg*

FRANCE: Abbes; Kaelberl, Lerond; Penverne, Lafont, Marcel;
Wisnieski, Douis, Kopa, Fontaine, Vincent.
GERMANY: Kwiatowski; Stollenwerk, Erhardt; Schnellinger,
Wewers, Szymaniak; Rahn, Sturm, Kelbassa, Schaefer,
Cieslarczyk.
SCORERS: Fontaine (4), Kopa, penalty, Douis for France;
Cieslarczyk, Rahn, Schaefer for Germany.

Final

BRAZIL 5, SWEDEN 2 (2-1). *Stockholm*

BRAZIL: Gilmar; Santos, D., Santos, N.; Zito, Bellini, Orlando;
Garrincha, Didì, Vavà, Pelé, Zagalo.
SWEDEN: Svensson; Bergmark, Axbom; Boerjesson, Gustavsson,
Parling; Hamrin, Gren, Simonsson, Liedholm, Skoglund.
SCORERS: Liedholm, Simonsson for Sweden; Vavà (2), Pelé (2),
Zagalo for Brazil.

2 THE BRAZILIAN TRIUMPH CONTINUES – DESPITE A RUDE INTERRUPTION BY ENGLAND

World Cup 1962 – held in Chile

It should, perhaps, have been held in Argentina. But if Chile had recently had earthquakes, then the general antipathy towards Argentina in footballing circles had not lessened. And as a spokesman for the Chilean claim put it, they needed the World Cup *'because* we have nothing'. Cunning logic indeed; and the Chileans set about building a new stadium in Santiago to house a hysterical populace. (Cynics pointed out Chile had won nothing since the Pacific War in the middle of the nineteenth century.)

Brazil were the favourites, inevitably. They had two new centre-backs; and that was all. Garrincha, Zagalo, Didì and Pelé were still there – though the last would play only two games before being replaced by another exciting striker in Amarildo. And taken seriously with the Brazilians were the Russians – who on a recent South American tour had beaten Argentina, Uruguay and Chile.

England had played well on their way to Chile, beating Peru 4-0 in Lima. In Greaves and Charlton they had world class forwards; in Bobby Moore, a debutant in Lima, a defender of poise. But the self-confidence was not there, the forwards would fail time and again to find a way through the packed defences that would make a nonsense of the early part of the competition.

Italy arrived with Gianni Rivera in their ranks, arguably one of the really gifted players Europe has seen since the end of the war. Eighteen then, a precision passer of the ball and with a

perfect sense of balance he would play one good game before
being dropped. The Italians also brought with them a host of
Oriundi – foreigners of Italian extraction – such as Altafini,
Sormani, Maschio and Sivori. A strong team on paper, but football matches are not won on paper – and the Italian campaign
would be catastrophic.

After a goalless draw against Germany, the Italians found
themselves involved in yet another of those World Cup 'battles'
when they came to play Chile in Santiago. At the root of the
trouble were some silly newspaper articles written by Italian
journalists, critical of the organisation of the tournament,
critical of the squalor of Santiago, critical of the morals of
Chilean womanhood. From the start of the game the Chileans
spat at the Italians, fouled them viciously. Ironic, therefore, that
the two players sent off in the game should both have been
Italian; while a left hook thrown by Sanchez, the Chilean
winger – one that broke Maschio's nose – went unseen by the
referee. Two-nil to Chile, and the Italians were effectively out of
the tournament.

Germany won that second group, with Schnellinger powerful
in defence, Seeler powerful in attack, Szymaniak destroying
everything in midfield. They had come up with a useful inside-
forward in Helmut Haller, who would find fame in Italy in later
years and compete in two further World Cups. And the Chileans,
inevitably, came through.

In group III, Brazil beat Mexico 2-0; were held to a goalless
draw by the unfancied Czechs – a game in which Pelé pulled a
muscle, and was lost to the rest of the tournament; then beat
Spain, with Amarildo – Pelé's replacement – getting both goals
in a 2-1 victory. The Czechs went through even though they had
lost one of their games, drawn another.

In group I, the Russians won a violent yet exciting game
against Yugoslavia 2-0; then were involved in an extraordinary
match against the Columbians, who after being 3-0 down in the
first fifteen minutes took the final score to 4-4. Yachin in goal
had a sad game, sad enough for some commentators to prophesy
the end of the greatest goalkeeper of modern times. Premature

indeed, if only for Yachin's fine displays in England four years later. Yugoslavia would go through to the quarter-finals with Russia, their little inside-forward, Sekularac, one of the men of the tournament.

And so to group IV, where the Hungarians looked a fine side. In Florian Albert they had unearthed a centre-forward of high gifts, another who would do marvellously in 1966. And in Solymosi, the right-half, they had a player of relaxed quality. These two were highly responsible for the 2-1 defeat of the English side in the first game; the 6-1 thrashing administered to Bulgaria in the second.

As for England, they played good football – with Bobby Charlton on great form – to defeat the Argentinians 3-1. Alan Peacock made his debut, and a fine one. But in the final game against the Bulgarians, the English could find no way through a massed defence, had to be content with a goalless draw. They were through, but few would dare to class them with the Hungarians.

In the event, they met – and were beaten by – Brazil. The 3-1 scoreline seemed slightly unjust; but Garrincha was in devastating form, seemingly having added to his vast repertoire of tricks the ability to head a ball viciously. And though Hitchens equalised for England before half-time, two mistakes by Springett in goal gave goals to Vavà and Amarildo after the interval.

No surprise, that result, but surprises elsewhere. Chile, for example, came through against Russia – with Yachin still inexplicably tense in goal, and the crowd manic in its joy. Not for the first or last time, the 'home' team had confounded early prognostication.

And Hungary went out. For eighty of the ninety minutes against the Czechs Hungary attacked, inflicting serious damage on the Czech crossbar and posts. Nothing, it seemed, would ever be a few millimetres farther in the right direction; and though Solymosi and Albert did everything that was asked of them, their team ever trailed to an early, thirteenth-minute goal from the Czech inside-forward, Scherer.

In the last quarter-final tie, the Yugoslavs put out the Germans. Only four minutes of the game remained when Galic, the inside-left, dribbled his way through the German defence and passed to Radakovic – head bandaged after a collision – to score. But the Germans could have had little reason for complaint. In Sekularac, the Yugoslavs had one of the best midfield players of the tournament; in Soskic a strong, agile goalkeeper; in Markovic, a commanding centre-back, who on the day would outplay the formidable Uwe Seeler.

In the semi-finals, it was the turn of Chile to fall before the devastating Garrincha. He scored the first of four Brazilian goals with a fierce left-foot shot, the second with another of his new-found trampoline-like headers. And though the Chileans hit back with a goal before half-time from Toro, two further goals – this time from Vavà – in the second half, and only a penalty in return, put the Brazilians through.

Not, however, without tremblings. In the second half of the game Garrincha himself was expelled for kicking retaliatorily at a Chilean opponent; and then suffered the indignity of having his head cut open by a bottle thrown from the crowd as he was leaving the pitch. In the event, the injury was not serious, the threat of suspension from the Final very real. It was said, how-ever, that the President of Brazil had listened to the game on headphones during Mass; that he had appealed personally to the disciplinary committee on Garrincha's behalf. The brilliant winger would play in the Final after receiving a caution.

The opposition to Brazil would be provided by the Czechs, victors in the other semi-final against Yugoslavia. As in the quarter-final, the Czechs had much less of the play; but this time took their chances well, scoring three goals, conceding one. Masopust controlled the midfield; the other two half-backs, Pluskal and Popluhar, sealed up the middle of the defence with rugged authority; Kvasniak ambled round in the forward line prompting and guiding. And the weary Yugoslavs were left to lose the match for third place, by the one goal and against a Chilean side again whipped on by a partisan crowd.

As in 1958, Brazil gave away the first goal of the Final –

Masopust scoring in the fourteenth minute after having run on to an exquisite through pass from Scherer; as in 1958, the team's reaction was swift and interesting. It was Pelé's replacement, Amarildo, who scored, running almost to the left-hand goal line with the ball, screwing an extraordinary shot past Schroiff, the Czech goalkeeper, who had positioned himself perfectly at the near post to narrow the angle.

One-one, then, at half-time; and when Brazil scored again in the sixty-ninth minute, good goal though it was, it came against the run of the play. Amarildo it was who collected a pass from Zito, cut past a defender and crossed for Zito himself to charge in and head just under the bar. Thus was the slightly one-paced elegance of Masopust and Kvasniak rewarded; and salt was further rubbed into the wound twelve minutes from time when Djalma Santos hooked a centre high into the Czech penalty area, Schroiff lost its flight against the glare of the sun, lost it when it hit the ground, and Vavà snapped in to score, 3-1, seemingly a convincing win; but Garrincha had been well controlled, Didì had been obscure.

Brazil had won the Cup for the second time, but with little of the flair that they had shown in Sweden. True, Pelé had been absent for the important games, and Pelé might have made a considerable difference. The Brazilians, however, had been forced to use Zagalo as a deep-lying winger, and the 4-2-4 formation of 1958 had wilted into the 4-3-3 of 1962, would even tempt people to think of four midfield players and only two genuine strikers.

More serious, it had been a disappointing tournament. The great Puskas, taking time off from scoring goals for his new club, Real Madrid, said of the football he had seen that it was 'war'. The qualifying games had provided a string of disappointments, defensive skill had been at a premium. The tournament in Sweden had provided 119 goals, that in Chile thirty less; and where Fontaine had scored so freely in 1958, the highest figure that any individual goalscorer would reach in Chile was four.

1962 – Final Stages

Quarter-Finals

YUGOSLAVIA 1, GERMANY 0 (0-0). *Santiago*
YUGOSLAVIA: Soskic; Durkovic, Jusufi; Radakovic, Markovic,
Popovic; Kovacevic, Sekularac, Jerkovic, Galic, Skoblar.
GERMANY: Fahrian; Novak, Schnellinger; Schultz, Erhardt,
Giesemann; Haller, Szymaniak, Seeler, Brulls, Schaefer.
SCORER: Radakovic for Yugoslavia.

BRAZIL 3, ENGLAND 1 (1-1). *Viña del Mar*

BRAZIL: Gilmar; Santos D., Mauro, Zozimo, Santos, N.; Zito,
Didì; Garrincha, Vavà, Amarildo, Zagalo.
ENGLAND: Springett; Armfield, Wilson; Moore, Norman,
Flowers; Douglas, Greaves, Hitchens, Haynes, Charlton.
SCORERS: Garrincha (2), Vavà for Brazil; Hitchens for England.

CHILE 2, RUSSIA 1 (2-1). *Arica*

CHILE: Escutti; Eyzaguirre, Contreras, Sanchez, R., Navarro;
Toro, Rojas; Ramirez, Landa, Tobar, Sanchez, L.
RUSSIA: Yachin; Tchokelli, Ostrovski; Voronin, Maslenkin,
Netto; Chislenko, Ivanov, Ponedelnik, Mamikin, Meshki.
SCORERS: Sanchez, L., Rojas for Chile; Chislenko for Russia.

CZECHOSLOVAKIA 1, HUNGARY 0 (1-0). *Rancagua*

CZECHOSLOVAKIA: Schroiff; Lala, Novak; Pluskal, Popluhar,
Masopust; Pospichal, Scherer, Kvasniak, Kadraba, Jelinek.
HUNGARY: Grosics; Matrai, Sarosi; Solymosi, Meszoly, Sipos;
Sandor, Rakosi, Albert, Tichy, Fenyvesi.
SCORER: Scherer for Czechoslovakia.

Semi-Finals

BRAZIL 4, CHILE 2 (2-1). *Santiago*

BRAZIL: Gilmar; Santos, D., Mauro, Zozimo, Santos, N.; Zito, Didì; Garrincha, Vavà, Amarildo, Zagalo.
CHILE: Escutti; Eyzaguirre, Contreras, Sanchez, R., Rodriguez; Toro, Rojas; Ramirez, Landa, Tobar, Sanchez, L.
SCORERS: Garrincha (2), Vavà (2), for Brazil; Toro, Sanchez, L. (penalty) for Chile.

CZECHOSLOVAKIA 3, YUGOSLAVIA 1 (0-0). *Vina del Mar*

CZECHOSLOVAKIA: Schroiff; Lala, Novak; Pluskal, Popluhar, Masopust; Pospichal, Scherer, Kvasniak, Kadraba, Jelinek.
YUGOSLAVIA: Soskic; Durkovic, Jusufi; Radakovic, Markovic, Popovic; Sujakovic, Sekularac, Jerkovic, Galic, Skoblar.
SCORERS: Kadraba, Scherer (2), for Czechoslovakia; Jerkovic for Yugoslavia.

Third Place Match

CHILE: Godoy; Eyzaguirre, Cruz, Sanchez, R., Rodriguez; Toro, Rojas; Ramirez, Campos, Tobar, Sanchez, L.
YUGOSLAVIA: Soskic; Durkovic, Svinjarevic; Radakovic, Markovic, Popovic; Kovacevic, Sekularac, Jerkovic, Galic, Skoblar.
SCORER: Rojas for Chile.

Final

BRAZIL 3, CZECHOSLOVAKIA 1 (1-1). *Santiago*

BRAZIL: Gilmar; Santos, D., Mauro, Zozimo, Santos, N.; Zito, Didì; Garrincha, Vavà, Amarildo, Zagalo.
CZECHOSLOVAKIA: Schroiff; Tichy, Novak; Pluskal, Popluhar, Masopust; Pospichal, Scherer, Kvasniak, Kadraba, Jelinek.
SCORERS: Masopust for Czechoslovakia; Amarildo, Zito, Vavà for Brazil.

World Cup 1966 – held in England

When he took over from Walter Winterbottom the managership of the English national side, Alf Ramsey promised that England would win the 1966 tournament. They did and he did; for there had been fewer stronger examples in the history of the game of 'the players' manager'. It was Nobby Stiles who said it after England had beaten Germany in the Final. '*You* did it, Alf,' he cried tearfully. 'We'd have been nothing without you.'

England had to be favourites, given home advantage, given a successful Scandinavian tour just before the series began. On paper they had a fine goalkeeper in Banks, a potential match-winner in Greaves, a gifted and well-drilled defence. But in midfield they relied on Bobby Charlton, always known as a striker. In the event Charlton would play superbly in the semi-final; be decisive in the Final. But those days were ahead.

Eyes also turned inevitably towards Brazil during their Scandinavian tour. But it was clear that the great days were passed. If Pelé was still there, threatening as ever, there were many questions that received unsatisfactory answers. Who would fill in for Zagalo, with his tireless and effective running? Who was there to replace the immaculate Didì? Was Garrincha sufficiently recovered from a car crash and a series of serious knee operations? In fact, so strange an amalgam was the Brazilian party between unproven young players and older hands that they brought with them the very two defenders they had omitted on grounds of old age four years earlier – Bellini and Orlando.

Russia still had Yachin, still lacked the spark that makes triumphant teams. The Italians had three stylish inside-forwards in Mazzola, Rivera and Bulgarelli, an accomplished goal-scoring back in the giant Facchetti. They had beaten Argentina 3-0 just before the competition opened. But they also had a reputation for playing below form away from home. And the Argentinians that day had fielded something of a reserve side.

The Germans still had the indomitable Seeler up front, the indestructible Schnellinger in defence. It was known that they

lacked a good goalkeeper, but had unearthed a fine young
attacking wing-half in Beckenbauer, still had Helmut Haller
to give guidance in midfield, and in Wolfgang Overath possessed
another midfield player of the highest skill and fierce ability to
read the patterns of a game.

The Brazilians were undoubtedly drawn in the toughest group
– against Bulgaria, Hungary and Portugal. They won the opening game, against the first of these three, lost the other two.
Against the Bulgarians both goals came from freekicks, a cannonball from Pelé, a 'banana' shot from Garrincha; and Pelé spent
much of the match trying to avoid scything tackles.

The Brazilians then came across Hungary, losers to Portugal
in their first game thanks to some desperately inefficient goalkeeping. (More than one authority thought that Hungary would
have won this competition had they been served in goal even
remotely well.) The Hungarians had Albert, one of their heroes
four years previously; they had a fine new forward in Bene, who
had played superbly in the winning 1964 Olympic team; they
had another hero from 1962 in Meszoly, always prepared to
break into attack from behind; and they had Farkas, a deadly
finisher close to goal.

Without Pelé, the Brazilians looked feeble indeed. Garrincha
looked creaky, the two elder statesmen of the defence – Djalma
Santos and Bellini – ominously static. Against fast and tricky
running, that Brazilian defence crumbled quickly. Bene swerved
and knifed through the middle after three minutes of play to slide
the ball home; and although Brazil equalised through the
young Tostao just before half-time, their goal came against all
justice.

It was in the second half that their fate was sealed. First
Albert ran through, slid the ball to Bene on the right, and
Farkas rushed in to smack home the volleyed cross – as spectacular a goal as the competition was to see. And then came a
penalty, tucked home by Meszoly. The Liverpool crowd rose
to the Hungarians, and particularly Albert; the Brazilians went
back to camp to plan survival against Portugal.

They did for this match what they might have done earlier –

play young men capable of running for ninety minutes. Pelé
came back clearly not fit, and was put out of the game early on
by a vicious tackle from Morais, one that failed to receive from
the too placid English referee the punishment it deserved –
expulsion. All those who saw it will never forget the sight of
Pelé, his face agonised, lying by the touchline swathed in a
blanket.

The game against Hungary had been Brazil's first defeat in a
World Cup match since 1954 – when they had been put out in
that infamous game – by the Hungarians. The Portugal game
showed that they deserved to be out. They had no answers to Albert,
Bene and Farkas; now they had no answers to the fast running
and powerful shooting of Eusebio. It was the famous coloured
player from Mozambique who smashed in a shot in the fourteenth minute – for Manga, the Brazilian goalkeeper to shovel
it away into the path of Simoes. A headed goal from Eusebio,
then a right-foot shot – and Brazil (despite Rildo's second-half
score) were out. They caught the train to Euston complaining –
rightly – of inefficient refereeing. But they had proved the point
that great teams are made up of great players, that greatness is
not bestowed magically from above to those countries who feel
they deserve it.

Elsewhere Argentina and West Germany came through from
group II, the former gathering a reputation for ruthlessness that
would serve to dim appreciation of their undoubted skills. Both
teams beat Switzerland and Spain, their game together was
drawn. The West Germans looked classy in a 5-0 victory over
Switzerland. They still had their own goalkeeping problems;
but the defence remained firm, the midfield enterprising. As for
Spain, they used their older players initially – and like Brazil
came to rue their choice. When they did put out their youngsters,
it was against the Germans and too late, despite a spirited performance.

England came through in the first group, desperately unconvincing. Against Uruguay they were unable to pierce the defensive
barrier; against Mexico it took a superb, spectacular shot from
long-distance and Bobby Charlton to break the deadlock; against

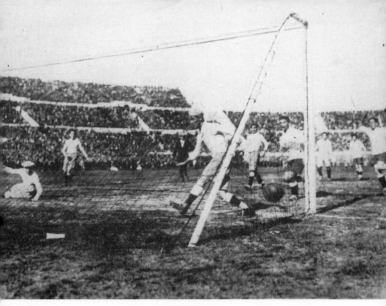

The last moments of the 1930 Final in which Uruguay beat Argentina 4-2, the scorer being Hector Castro (just to the left of the right-hand upright), who was known as 'El Manco' after his right arm had been amputated at the elbow.

The only goal of the Semi-final in the 1934 World Cup in which Italy beat Austria, scored by Enrico Guiata. Italy went on to win the Final against Czechoslovakia 2-1 after extra time had been played.

Italy triumph again in 1938 by beating Hungary 4-2. Holding the Jules Rimet trophy is their manager, Vittorio Pozzo, and just to *his* left is Silvio Piola, who scored twice in the Final.

The 1950 World Cup and Uruguay's goalkeeper, Roque Maspoli, manages to dive down to the ball before Brazil's forward, Ademir, can reach it. Uruguay won the match 2-1, although Brazil had 'home' advantage, and thus took the title for the second time.

Max Morlock (West Germany) slides the ball under the arms of the advancing Hungarian goalkeeper, Gyula Grosics, to score his side's first goal in the 'unexpected' 3-2 victory in the 1954 Final.

Harry Gregg (Northern Ireland) fails to stop a shot by Uwe Seeler (West Germany), in a group match from the 1958 World Cup which finished in a 2-2 draw.

Kalle Svensson dives to prevent trouble from John Charles during the goalless draw in the 1958 tournament between Sweden and Wales.

From the 1958 Final. The electrifying Garrincha centres for Vavà to strike home Brazil's first, and equalising, goal in the 5-2 defeat of Sweden.

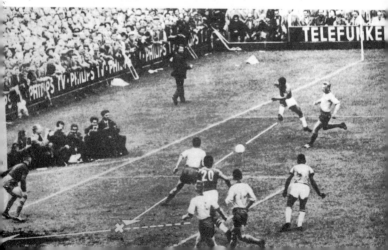

Luis Suarez (Spain) trying to find a way through an uncompromising Czechoslovakian defence during the 1962 World Cup, which his side lost just by the one goal. Czechoslovakia proceeded to the Final.

The Brazilian team before the 1962 Final in which they beat Czechoslovakia 3-1. *Top (left to right):* Djalma Santos, Zito, Gilmar, Mauro, Nilton Santos and Zozimo. *Bottom:* Garrincha, Didi, Vavà, Amarildo and Zagalo.

Brazil against Hungary in 1966 and Jairzinho attempts a header which the Hungarian goalkeeper, Jozsef Gelei, manages to save. It was a memorable match which Hungary won 3-1.

Russia versus Hungary Quarter-final in 1966 which Russia won 2-1. Here Ferenc Bene (second from left) scores Hungary's only goal.

1966 Quarter-final between England and Argentina. Referee Kreitlen orders off Antonio Rattin after he had objected to the 'booking' of a colleague. Play was held up for ten minutes in which time the Argentinians petitioned, argued and at one time appeared ready to leave the field *en masse*.

Third Place match in 1966 between Portugal and Russia. Eusebio (Portugal) forces his way through the Russian defence only to see his shot saved by Lev Yachin. Despite this, Portugal won 2-1 and Eusebio finished as the highest scorer in the tournament.

1966 Final and Wolfgang Weber scores in the final minute of normal time. Also in the picture are Uwe Seeler, George Cohen, Bobby Moore, Ray Wilson, Kurt Schnellinger, Jackie Charlton and Gordon Banks (the goalkeeper).

Geoff Hurst (England) makes sure of victory in the 1966 Final by driving home the fourth goal in England's 4-2 victory over West Germany. The German player is Wolfgang Overath.

France they looked unconvincing against a team down to ten
men for much of the game. The English defence, however, appeared impressive; fortunately indeed to have a goalkeeper of
Banks' class in a year of so much bad goalkeeping. The Uruguayans beat France, drew with Mexico, to join them.

Up in the North-east it was nearly all Russia. They disposed
of North Korea in the opening game, scoring three goals in the
process; then scored just the one goal against a lethargic Italian
team bereft of Rivera's skills. As so often Italian caution in team
selection and tactics brought its just rewards. But they still had
to play North Korea – a game that should have given them little
cause for sleeplessness.

In the event, the game was as big a shock as England's defeat
at the hands of the Americans sixteen years earlier. Though the
Italians lost Bulgarelli in the thirty-fourth minute with strained
ligaments (an injury caused by his own foul tackle), they
throughout played like ghosts. Pak Doo Ik it was who scored the
only goal of the match just before half-time, and when the final
whistle came, the Middlesbrough crowd rushed on to the pitch
in joy. Who could ever forget the sight of one enormous British
sailor tucking a Korean player under each arm and rushing round
the pitch like a lunatic. As for the Italians they went home in
shame, were pelted with rotten vegetables on arrival at Genoa
airport at the dead of night.

Two of the quarter-finals remain memorable – and for totally
differing reasons. The Russians won by the odd goal in three
against the Hungarians, manifestly less imaginative, but having
in goal a Yachin instead of a Gelei; and at Sheffield the West
Germans won 4-0 against a dispirited and disorganised Uruguayan
team that had two men sent off and never really tried to stay in
the game.

London and Liverpool would see the more fascinating
matches. For their game against Argentina at Wembley,
England left out the injured Jimmy Greaves (and were perhaps
glad to do so, for his form had been disappointing) and brought
in Geoff Hurst – whose last game, against Denmark, had been
disastrously uninspiring. As so often happens in these things,

Hurst turned out to be the match-winner, scoring the only goal of the game thirteen minutes from time; and once forcing Roma, the Argentinian goalkeeper, to an acrobatic windmill-like save at point-blank range.

Everything, however, came to be overshadowed in most people's minds by the events just before half-time when Rattin, the South Americans' captain, was sent off by the German referee, Herr Kreitlin, for objecting to the booking of one of his team mates. Rattin himself had been booked for a trip on Bobby Charlton; but though there had been many nasty and cynical Argentinian fouls, that particular one had been by no means the worst. Later the referee claimed to have sent off Rattin 'for the look on his face'. In the event the game was held up for eleven minutes while Rattin refused to move, while the Argentinian coach, Juan Carlos Lorenzo argued from the touchline, while officials tried to get the game restarted. So the Argentinians lost the most effective player in midfield; and there can be little doubt that had they initially gone out to play as well as they could, the result might have been very different. Certainly England's eleven players made heavy work of the game in the second half against ten opponents bent merely on destructive tactics.

After the game officials moved quickly to protect the referee against the Argentinian reserves, who joined their colleagues to pound on the door of the English dressing-room, to make insinuating gestures and statements to World Cup officials. One of their players urinated on the floor outside the English quarters, their manager rubbed forefinger and thumb meaningfully together, and Alf Ramsey was distressed enough to refer to them as 'animals' in a remark that he later – understandably grudgingly – was forced to withdraw.

England were through, the mundanity of their play masked by events off the ball. And in the semi-finals they would meet Portugal, winners against the North Koreans in a game as extraordinary as that at Wembley. After their bizarre and heart-warming achievements against the Italians, the Koreans took on Eusebio and his men, nipping about smartly. A goal

in the first minute was a fine tonic; two more soon after and the
fancied Portuguese were three down.

That was the point at which Eusebio must have realised that
Nemesis was staring him in the face. He ran through for one
goal, smashed home a penalty after Torres had had his legs taken
from underneath him, added two further goals in the second half.
Augusto got a fifth, from a corner, and the Koreans were finally
forced out, having given vast entertainment, having puzzled
everyone as to the nature of their achievement. Everyone knew
that for months they had lived in solitary and rigorous confinement. But the quickness with which they had learnt made many
people wonder whether future competitions wouldn't deserve
greater participation on the part of teams drawn from those
countries with little footballing tradition.

Given the magnificent way in which Lancashire – and
particularly Liverpool – had supported its games in the competition, Liverpudlians deserved much better than they received
from the Russia–Germany semi-final, little more nor less than a
war of attrition. Sabo made a potentially vicious tackle on Beckenbauer – only to come away limping himself; a long-range
sliding effort from Schnellinger on Chislenko left that Russian
limping. He went off for treatment, returned, lost a ball to Held,
chased the German and was rightly sent off by Concetto Lo
Bello, the famous Italian referee. Haller it was who scored the
first German goal a minute before half time, just after Schnellinger's tackle; and Beckenbauer curled a shot around the Russian
defensive wall for the second. Porkujan replied for Russia, but
too late. And although the Russian manager publicly blamed
Yachin for the two German goals, the truth was that without him
they might have ceded two or three in the first twenty minutes.

The England–Portugal semi-final provided a pleasant and
enthralling contrast. It was in this game that the English really
came together to look formidable, the defence strong as ever,
Bobby Charlton stupendous in midfield and behind the attack
in a performance that must have gone a long way to earning him
the award as European Footballer of the Year. Everything he
tried, and he tried everything, came off. His swerving runs, long

passing, ferocious shooting – all were in evidence. He it was who
scored the first goal, after José Pereira had pushed out a shot
from Hunt; and just as important, every Portuguese player he
passed on the way back to the centre circle stopped to shake his
hand.

From first whistle to last the game was played at an electrifying pace, graced by electric skills. There was the battle
between Torres and Jack Charlton, two giants in the air; that
between Stiles and Eusebio, with the heart and guts of the
former matched against the amazing skills of the latter; and there
was the battle in midfield between Charlton and the Portuguese
captain, Coluna, with his casual talent for passing, his instinctual
reading of the game. When Hurst raced through eleven minutes
from the end and cut the ball back from the by line for Charlton
to hammer in his second goal, that seemed that. But three
minutes later Jack Charlton was forced to give away a penalty,
taken and scored by Eusebio. And the last few minutes were
played out in a frenzy – Stiles making a fine last-ditch tackle on
Simoes, Banks going down brilliantly to a vicious shot from
Coluna. England were through to the Final; and though Eusebio
left the pitch in tears, comforted by his team mates, he would
have the consolation (admittedly small) of scoring in Portugal's
victory over Russia for the third place match, and thus consoli-
date his position as the tournament's leading scorer.

The Final would prove as dramatic as the changes in the
weather – now brilliant sunshine, now driving rain; certainly
the most dramatic Final that the competition has ever seen. It
was the Germans who took the lead – in the thirteenth minute
after Ray Wilson – normally so cool at fullback – had non-
chalantly headed a loose ball down to the feet of Haller, for the
German inside-forward to slide the ball past Banks. It was a lead
Germany would hold for only six minutes – until Hurst turned
in a free-kick taken too swiftly by Bobby Moore.

It was eighteen minutes into the second-half before England
took the lead. For much of the match Alan Ball had run Schnellinger ragged – Schnellinger, thought of by many as the best
fullback in the world. Time after time Ball had forced him away

from his touchline and into the middle, where he had been
manifestly less assured. Now the small, red-haired England
'winger' forced and took a corner. The ball came to Hurst, who
shot – only for a German defender to block and Peters to clip
the rebound past Tilkowski, the German goalkeeper.

Pressing increasingly towards attack, the Germans were
leaving themselves vulnerable in defence. Three minutes from
what should have been the end of the game Hunt burst through,
passed too shallowly to Charlton – whose shot was tame. And in
the last minute, agonisingly, the Germans equalised. The referee
deemed Jack Charlton to have obstructed Held (many thought
the offence inverted), Emmerich drove the kick powerfully
through the England wall, and when Held touched the ball on,
Weber – the centre-half – rushed in to score.

Thus to extra-time, with both teams exhausted apart from
Alan Ball, seemingly ready to run for many hours yet. Ten
minutes into the first period he scampered off down the right
wing and crossed precisely – for Hurst to smash a shot against
the underside of the crossbar. We can now say that it was
probably not a goal. But to establish that fact it took a lot of
people many hours of very hard work in cinema laboratories all
over the world. At the time the referee conferred with linesman –
the Russian Bakhramov – and the most contentious goal of a
World Cup final was allowed.

In the last minutes, with England having hung on bravely,
Hurst it was again who ran through a demoralised and static
German defence to slash in a fierce shot with his left foot. He
had done what no one had done before, scored a hat trick in a
Final. And England, though far from being the most stylish or
interesting team of the competition, had done what Alf Ramsey
had said they would. They would have their critics, and many
would complain about the incompetence and lack of sensibility
in much of the refereeing. But the competition had been the best
organised and best supported of any, and England's games in
semi-final and Final worthy to set with the best in the history of
the World Cup tournament.

1966 – Final Stages

Quarter-Finals

ENGLAND 1, ARGENTINA 0 (0-0). *Wembley*

ENGLAND: Banks (Leicester City); Cohen (Fulham), Wilson
(Everton); Stiles (Manchester United), Charlton, J. (Leeds
United), Moore (West Ham United); Ball (Blackpool), Hurst
(West Ham United), Charlton, R. (Manchester United), Hunt
(Liverpool), Peters (West Ham United).
ARGENTINA: Roma; Ferreiro, Perfumo, Albrecht, Marzolini;
Gonzalez, Rattin, Onega; Solari, Artime, Mas.
SCORER: Hurst for England.

WEST GERMANY 4, URUGUAY 0 (1-0). *Sheffield*

WEST GERMANY: Tilkowski; Hottges, Weber, Schultz, Schnellinger; Beckenbauer, Haller, Overath; Seeler, Held, Emmerich.
URUGUAY: Mazurkiewiez; Troche; Ubinas, Gonçalves, Manic-
era, Caetano; Salva, Rocha, Silva, Cortez, Perez.
SCORERS: Held, Beckenbauer, Seeler, Haller for West Germany.

PORTUGAL 5, NORTH KOREA 3. (2-3) *Everton*

PORTUGAL: José Pereira; Morais, Baptista, Vicente, Hilario;
Graça, Coluna, Augusto; Eusebio, Torres, Simoes.
NORTH KOREA: Ri Chan Myung; Rim Yung Sum, Shin Yung
Kyoo, Ha Jung Wong, O Yook Kyung; Pak Seung Jin, Jon
Seung Hwi; Han Bong Jin, Pak Doo Ik, Li Dong Woon, Yang
Sung Kook.
SCORERS: Pak Seung Jin, Yang Sung Kook, Li Dong Woon for
North Korea; Eusebio 4 (2 penalties), Augusto for Portugal.

RUSSIA 2, HUNGARY 1 (1-0) *Sunderland*

RUSSIA: Yachin; Ponomarev, Chesternjiev, Voronin, Danilov;
Sabo, Khusainov; Chislenko, Banichevski, Malafeev, Porkujan.
HUNGARY: Gelei; Matrai; Kaposzta, Meszoly, Sipos, Szepesi;
Nagy, Albert, Rakosi; Bene, Farkas.
SCORERS: Chislenko, Porkujan for Russia; Bene for Hungary.

Semi-Finals

WEST GERMANY 2, RUSSIA 1(1-0). *Everton*

WEST GERMANY: Tilkowski; Hottges, Weber, Schultz, Schnell-
inger; Beckenbauer, Haller, Overath, Seeler, Held, Emmerich.
RUSSIA: Yachin; Ponomarev, Chesternjiev, Voronin, Danilov;
Sabo, Khusainov; Chislenko, Banichevski, Malafeev, Porkujan.
SCORERS: Haller, Beckenbauer for Germany; Porkujan for
Russia.

ENGLAND 2, PORTUGAL 1 (1-0). *Wembley*

ENGLAND: Banks (Leicester City); Cohen (Fulham), Wilson
(Everton); Stiles (Manchester United), Charlton, J. (Leeds
United), Moore (West Ham United); Ball (Blackpool), Hurst
(West Ham United), Charlton, R. (Manchester United), Hunt
(Liverpool), Peters (West Ham United).
PORTUGAL: José Pereira; Festa, Baptista, Carlos, Hilario; Graça,
Coluna, Augusto; Eusebio, Torres, Simoes.
SCORERS: Charlton, R. (2) for England; Eusebio (penalty) for
Portugal.

Third Place Match

PORTUGAL 2, RUSSIA 1 (1-1). *Wembley*
PORTUGAL: José Pereira; Festa, Baptista, Carlos, Hilario; Graça,
Coluna, Augusto; Eusebio, Torres, Simoes.
RUSSIA: Yachin; Ponomarev, Khurtsilava, Korneev, Danilov;
Voronin, Sichinava; Metreveli, Malafeev, Banichevski, Sere-
brianikov.
SCORERS: Eusebio (penalty), Torres for Portugal; Malafeev for
Russia.

Final

ENGLAND 4, WEST GERMANY 2 (1-1) (2-2) after extra
time. *Wembley*
ENGLAND: Banks; Cohen, Wilson; Stiles, Charlton, J., Moore;
Ball, Hurst, Charlton, R., Hunt, Peters.
WEST GERMANY: Tilkowski; Hottges, Schultz; Weber, Schnell-
inger, Haller; Beckenbauer, Overath, Seeler, Held, Emmerich.
SCORERS: Hurst (3), Peters for England; Haller, Weber for
Germany.

World Cup 1970 – held in Mexico

Given that the tournament tended to be played alternately in
Europe and South America, it was inevitable that Mexico would
be a venue sooner or later. For many, however, the 'later' would
have been preferable. The 1968 Olympiad had shown precisely
and agonisingly the problems thrown up in expecting top-class
athletes to compete at high altitudes. And few parts of central
Mexico were at less than 6–7,000 feet above sea level. The non-
chalant could at least pretend that it made life more interesting.

What could have been prevented – and wasn't – was the
callous selling-out of the tournament to financial interests. Too
many games were played in noonday heat – merely to satisfy
European television companies eager to televise games at peak

viewing times. England, for example, played their vital group match against Brazil at noon, in temperatures of nearly 100 degrees and there was barely an England player who had not lost eight or ten pounds in weight as a result of dehydration.

England's preparations had been thorough enough. The team arrived in Mexico well before the tournament started; good accommodation had been found; supplies of food and drink had been flown out (though the Mexican customs officials appeared un-cooperative at first); the players were even supplied with reading material by Coronet Books, one of the country's leading paperback publishing firms. Leaving Mexico for a short tour, England won handsome victories over Columbia and Ecuador, the defence seemingly as ungenerous as it had been in 1966.

It was after the second of these games, as the team stopped off in Bogota on the way back to Mexico that Bobby Moore, the English captain, was absurdly accused of having stolen a bracelet from a hotel jewellers. Much has been written about this extra-ordinary incident, that would last for nearly two years, until the 'charges' were finally dropped. The important point to underline is Moore's amazing coolness during the whole affair. In a situation where many players might have cracked under the nervous strain imposed by being unable to fly back to Mexico with the rest of the team, of having to remain in a state of semi-solitary confinement while the matter was tentatively cleared up Moore was simply magnificent. Within days he was to go out and prove to the world that, as in 1966, he remained the best defensive wing-half in modern football.

If England had Moore, then Brazil still had Pelé. The Brazil-ians had taken, only months before the Finals, the extraordinary step of sacking their manager, the bubbling Joao Saldanha, and replacing him with Mario Zagalo, one of the heroes of 1958 and 1962. No one doubted the Brazilian talent. If they had a goal-keeper of laughable mediocrity in Felix, if their defence seemed unsound – then they had Gerson in midfield and up front Jair-zinho and Tostao. The latter had recently undergone eye surgery, but was known to be a formidable foil to Pelé. The first few games would tell all about Brazil.

The West Germans were there also, eager for the chance to revenge their defeat at the hands of the English four years previously. The bulk of that side remained, they had two incisive wingers in Grabowski and Libuda, a 'new' goalkeeper in Maier, one of the best of the tournament. And that is not meant disparagingly. One of the many contrasts between the 1966 competition and that to be held in Mexico would be the overall improvement in goalkeeping standards. Banks (England), Kavazashvili (Russia), Piot (Belgium), Calderon (Mexico), Albertosi (Italy) and Mazurkiewicz (Uruguay) – all, with Maier, kept goal well in conditions that were far from helpful, ones in which the ball moved fast through the rarefied air, swerving and dipping unexpectedly, ones in which the brightness of the light put a premium on good judgement. We might note here that the fearsome Gerd Muller, who would score most goals in the tournament, came to face only two of the above-mentioned, when Germany played their semi-final against Italy and their final game against Uruguay.

The Italians came strangely, having qualified with some ease against East Germany and Wales in their preliminary group. In Riva they had a striker of renown, his left foot a terrifying weapon when given the chance to exercise itself. But too often Riva's brilliant goals had camouflaged weaknesses in the defence, lack of understanding in midfield. Mazzola was there for the second time, Rivera for the third – both players of high technical accomplishment, and supposedly unable to play together. The Italians decided in favour of the *staffeta*, a system whereby Mazzola would play the first half of each game, Rivera the second. The latter found it unacceptable, said so loudly, was nearly sent home as punishment, stayed, and in two games at least, would prove that he is one of the world's great intuitive players.

The Russians looked solid as ever, with Kavazashvili a worthy successor in goal to the great Yachin, and Shesternev a sweeper little behind Bobby Moore in terms of technical expertise and tactical acumen. They had an interesting young striker in Bishovets, but would play a type of football that lacked genuine inventiveness. Uruguay were another team strong on paper, again served brilliantly in goal (by Mazurkiewicz, one of the very small clutch of good goalkeepers four years previously), and with some terrifyingly robust defenders. One remembers particularly Montero Castillo in the centre of the field, Ubinas and Ancheta elsewhere. And the joker in the pack had to be Peru, coached for the tournament by Didì, the Brazilian ex-player and perennial hero of 1954, 1958 and 1962. It was known that they had some forwards of dazzling technical gifts, but did they have a team, could they put together a game?

Generally speaking those teams that were expected to come through, came through. The first game of the first group – and the tournament – was that between Mexico (the hosts) and Russia. A goalless draw, as with its 1966 counterpart, sounded an ominous warning. But Belgium played some light, waltzing football to beat El Salvador the following day; and when they came to meet Russia, deserved better than the 4-1 defeat that they allowed to be inflicted upon them. Bishovets scored two of those goals, Shesternev marshalled the defence superbly; and it was one of those days when the Russians showed the world just what they could do when prepared to cast off thoughts of weighty preparation and over-drilled tactics. And in the final game of the group, the Mexicans went through against the Belgians 1-0, thanks to a hotly disputed penalty decision, one that seemed to have been not uninfluenced by the frenzy of a vast home crowd. Mexico, unconvincingly, and Russia through, then, from that group.

Group II looked good for both Italy and Uruguay. Israel looked too raw, Sweden – despite the presence of one or two players of high talent, such as Kindvall and Grahn, who played their club football outside Sweden – lacked strength in depth. They it was who first faced Italy, going down to a drive from some long range delivered by the Italian midfield player, Domenghini, who throughout the tournament would play with a ubiquity that perilously ignored the heat of the sun and the rarity of the air. The Uruguayans scraped through 2-0 against Israel, more importantly lost Pedro Rocha, their midfield general after only a few minutes of play. It was an injury that would force the South

American team even further back on to their defensive and
uncompromising heels, for Rocha would take no further part in
the tournament.

The next match brought these two teams together into a
goalless draw, with both sets of players full of hostility (both
masked and overt). Riva was to claim that from the first Uruguayan defenders had spat at him whenever they were close;
which did not excuse his lethargy. More dreary football was to
follow, and the results continued to prove evidence of the essentially defensive attitudes that permeated group matches. The
Swedes beat the Uruguayans, who went through on a marginally
better goal average; and the Italians got through with two goalless
draws and that one win. Top of the group with only one goal in
three matches: that, surely, couldn't be the stuff of which world
champions were made?

Group III was, indubitably, the toughest on paper; and
certainly the matches from that group provided some of the
most fascinating football. If the English won their first game
against Rumania, they did so with some lack of ease, thanks to a
goal from Geoff Hurst in the seventieth minute, and despite
some sadistic tackling by the Rumanian defenders, a certain
Mocanu in particular. If the Brazilians appeared to thrash the
Czechs 4-1, it must be remembered that Petras scored the first
goal of the match for Czechoslovakia, that they were served with
some indifferent goalkeeping, that the third Brazilian goal
(scored by Jairzinho) looked suspiciously offside. But Pelé was
on superb form, scored an extraordinary goal; Rivelino put
another in from a swerving free-kick; Jairzinho scored again,
always threatened when he had possession; and Gerson in midfield sprayed accurate passes around with high panache, underlining the thought that so many of the world's finest distributors
have been players whose athleticism was far from robust. Gerson,
for example, is something of a one-paced player (and that pace
never faster than slow-medium) who is a compulsive cigarette
smoker. Hardly the stuff of which the textbook heroes are made,
but a player of great influence.

Too many people – and particularly in England – have tended

to overlook the fact of Gerson's absence when England came to
play Brazil. That is not to say that England didn't play
thoroughly well, that they did not suggest themselves as one of
the two or three best teams of the tournament during that game.
It was a classic, worthy to enter the Pantheon of brilliant World
Cup games. The English had gone to Mexico in the rôle of
villains, with too many people disgruntled as to the manner of
their victory four years earlier; and this animosity was to mani-
fest itself at every turn. The night before the Brazil game a crowd
several thousand strong milled round the Hilton Hotel, where
they were staying, and contrived to make enough noise to
prevent the players getting any sleep. Many admitted after-
wards that they had for long minutes and hours simply stood
by the windows of their rooms, staring at the crowd below,
and at the inability of the Mexican police to deal with the
problem.

They then went out at midday, in scorching heat that
approached 100 degrees of Fahrenheit and played Brazil off the
pitch for long stretches of the game. Mullery played brilliantly,
policing Pelé with scrupulous toughness. True, Pelé got away
from him in the early minutes of the game after Jairzinho had
rounded Cooper on England's left and smacked across a perfect
centre; up went Pelé, down came the ball, and down also came
Gordon Banks to scoop the ball up with his right wrist – a save
that must rank with the very best in the history of the World
Cup tournament. Otherwise Pelé was kept moderately quiet;
and Moore at the heart of the defence gave further evidence that
he was the best defensive player in the world, his timing of the
tackle precise, his reading of the game astute, his distribution
imaginative.

The only goal of the match (perfect evidence that goals in
themselves do not exciting football make) came after fourteen
minutes of the second half, after Tostao had teased the left of the
English defence and slid the ball across goal for Jairzinho to
score. The truth was, however, that if Banks was forced to at
least three other saves of high quality, England were given, and
missed, a plentitude of chances at the other end. Ball hit the bar,

missed another good chance; Astle blazed wide after being put into an attractive position; Hurst might have had a goal, but shot feebly at the crucial moment. If the style is the man, then the style must also be the game; and yet again we were left to ponder that one of the essential weaknesses of the English game was its lack of high technical accomplishment – where the world's best strikers would snap up chances with glee, too often English forwards had not the basic 'killer' instinct that comes hand in hand (or foot to foot) with technical prowess.

The Brazilians went on to beat the Rumanians, again despite the deprivation of Gerson; and, on this occasion, that of Rivelino. England drafted in a handful of 'reserves' for the game against the Czechs, played badly, won through a disputed penalty; and joined Brazil in the quarter-finals.

In group IV were the mysterious Peruvians. In their first game, they fell behind to Bulgaria, conceded two goals from set pieces; and then in the second half turned on their skills. Many were quick to compare them with the Brazilians in their flamboyance, their brilliant control. In defence they had a sturdy player in Chumpitaz, some imaginative forwards in Gallardo, Sotil, Cubillas and Baylon; and in the space of twenty minutes turned the two-goal deficit into a 3-2 score that would last until the game's finish.

That would prove to be the decisive game in the group. For although they fared poorly against Morocco in their first match, the West Germans seemed certainties for qualification; a thought that was reinforced when they came to play the Bulgarians in turn. Though the East Europeans scored first through Nikodimov (following a free kick), the Germans ran in five goals, three of them going to Muller. Libuda was on venomous form on their right, Muller and Seeler brave and energetic in the middle. In fact Muller would score another hat trick when the Germans came to meet Peru a few days later, marching firmly along the road that would make him the tournament's highest scorer. Despite that 3-1 defeat, Peru would qualify.

No goal Muller scored in the competition was, however, more important than that he slashed home in the quarter-final tie that followed, when the Germans were drawn against England. It was a game England could, and should, have won. For a team of their defensive prowess to lead by two clear goals and eventually lose by the odd score in five was remarkable. It is too easy to blame Peter Bonetti, drafted into the goalkeeping position after Banks had been forced to withdraw with a stomach complaint of mysterious origin. Banks may well have saved two of the three German goals to be scored; but there were other, better reasons to explain the collapse.

England's lead came through Mullery – racing through to exchange passes with Lee, sliding the ball out to Newton on the right, smashing home the perfect cross; and Peters – knocking in another fine cross from Newton. That left England two up after five minutes of the second half, and seemingly set for a good win. And then came the substitutions – Grabowski on for Libuda; Bell and Hunter on for Charlton and Peters – that were to prove decisive. While Charlton remained, Beckenbauer, his policeman, stayed quiet; without further patrolling duties, Beckenbauer cut loose, scored the first, important, German goal. Where Cooper had controlled Libuda on the left, he now found Grabowski irrepressible. Although Hurst nearly made the score 3-1 with a fine low header, it was the Germans who came through, Seeler backheading a long cross from Schnellinger.

As in the 1966 Final, the game between the two countries entered extra time, with the crowd noisily pro-German, and England's defence looking increasingly tired. Hurst scored – to be given, mysteriously, offside. And then came the deciding goal – Grabowski winning control on the right, punting over a cross, which Muller tucked away as the ball was nodded down to him. England were out of the competition, after having controlled vast stretches of their games against Brazil and West Germany, after having suggested themselves strongly as possible opposition for Brazil in the Final.

Through into the semi-finals with Germany would go Italy, Brazil and Uruguay. The last won through in the final moments of extra time in a hard game against the Russians, and with a hotly disputed goal into the bargain. But the Russians had missed too many chances to have reason for bitter complaint.

Brazil went through, now with both Rivelino and Gerson back in the side, and at the expense of Peru to the tune of 4-2. Gallardo scored two goals for the entertaining Peruvians, but they were up against a side that knew their own footballing language and were more adept practitioners.

And Italy went through, stuttering for much of their game against Mexico, until Gianni Rivera made his appearance at the start of the second half and suggested openings for his compatriots. Riva scored twice, delighting those who knew his prowess and were still waiting patiently for evidence of its existence; and there was a goal from Rivera himself, nice ammunition for those who felt that Italy were squandering his exquisite talents, that there should always have been a place for him in that team, with or without the brave resourceful Sandro Mazzola.

The semi-final draw – Brazil against Uruguay, Italy against West Germany – promised, and delivered, much. The first of these games pitted the resource of the Brazilian midfield and attack against the misanthropy of the Uruguayan defence, with its squad of muscular central defenders. In the event, it was Uruguay who scored first, through Cubilla (as opposed to Cubillas, the Peruvian), and though Brazil equalised just before half time through Clodoaldo, the important second goal did not materialise until fourteen minutes before the end, when Jairzinho danced past three defenders on the right and drove the ball home from a sharp angle. A goal from Rivelino in the last second of the game gave the scoreline a lopsided quality that was grossly unfair to the courage and ingenuity of much of the Uruguayan play, still deprived of the skills of the injured – and potentially influential – Pedro Rocha.

But Italy against West Germany – that was really something of a collector's item. It was an interesting comment on the Italian footballing mentality that after a game of thrilling interest, despite the fact that their team had been victorious, many Italian commentators would dismiss it as being something of a circus turn on the grounds that neither of the two defences was good enough. In fact, Italy created much of their good fortune

early in the game when a bad tackle by Bertini left the elegant
Beckenbauer with an injured arm. He would play much of the
game at strolling pace and in some pain, his arm strapped to
his chest.

The Italians took the lead after only seven minutes, Boninsegna clearing Riva out of his way to plant a left-footed shot firmly
past Maier. Given the Italian penchant for defensive expertise,
the Germans must have known that they had a titanic struggle
on their hands, and well though they played against the cautious
Italians in the second half, too many chances went begging.
Indeed it was not until the third minute of injury time that
Schnellinger, the German sweeper (and ironically he served
brilliantly in that rôle at club level for A.C. Milan), came forward
to slide the ball home after Grabowski had crossed from the left.

Into extra-time, and on came the nervousness and the mistakes.
The Germans went ahead after five minutes through Muller;
Burgnich came up to knock in Rivera's free kick; Riva scored
a fine goal with that formidable left foot of his – and the first
period of extra-time ended with Italy leading 3-2. The Italians
were pulled back again soon after the resumption of play, when
Muller dived low to head home; and then came the decisive
goal, with the talented Boninsegna taking the ball out to the left,
leaving his opponent Schulz on his bottom, and crossing for
Gianni Rivera to drive the ball precisely into goal. Once again
Rivera had missed the first forty-five minutes; once again he
had been decisive in the later stages of a game. The Italians were
through, not remotely the second best side in the tournament,
but undoubtedly one of high technical accomplishment, and
in that semi-final game, having given the lie to those
detractors eager to claim that Italian teams always lack fire and
spirit.

In the play-off for third place the Germans did what the
Italians had failed to do – and beat Uruguay. They did so with a
fine goal scored by Overath after a thrilling movement that involved Libuda, Muller and Seeler. There was entertaining action
at both ends, with Mazurkiewicz and Walter (the young German
goalkeeper) both being forced to fine saves. But a match of

technical adroitness could not raise the crowd – which, like the televised world, awaited the Final itself.

Brazil won it, and won it handsomely. They did so with football of assured fluency, they did it by underlining brilliantly, and against the master exponents of defensive football, all the old clichés about attack being the best means of defence. Of the Italians Sandro Mazzola covered vast tracts of ground, played with authority and spirit; Boninsegna showed what a dangerous striker he could be, given even a few metres of space; Facchetti strove manfully against Jairzinho. But much of the marking was sloppy on the one hand, crude on the other; and there was about the team as a whole a curious refusal to play with any real vestige of self-confidence.

It was, fittingly, Pelé who gave the Brazilians the lead after eighteen minutes, heading down Rivelino's cross; if the great man had a comparatively human game, then his presence and brilliance had given the tournament as a whole a fine streak of class. And no one looked more bemused than he when the Italians equalised a few minutes before half-time through Boninsegna and after a silly back-pass by Clodoaldo had left Felix stranded outside the Brazilian goal.

That was delusion indeed, for in the second half, the Brazilians made heavy amends. Gerson, who throughout played with a majesty that capitalised on the failure of the Italian midfield, was the scorer of the second of the four Brazilian goals, his left foot curling in a fine shot from distance. Jairzinho it was who scored the third, slipping in a pass from Pelé and setting a new record by virtue of having scored in all six games in which he played; and the Italians were a thoroughly demoralised side by the time Carlos Alberto came through down the right touchline to crash the ball in after an exquisitely weighted pass from Pelé had put him through in the last few minutes of the game.

The Italians brought on Juliano for the ineffectual Bertini; with six minutes to go, bizarrely substituted Rivera for Boninsegna – a move that was staggering in its lack of logic. Had Rivera appeared earlier, in place of the tired Domenghini, one might have seen the point, he might have effected something of a

rescue. But the ship had been truly sunk; despite their appearance in the Final the Italians would go home and indulge in the
most Machiavellian post-mortems. And by virtue of their third
victory, the Brazilians would appropriate the Jules Rimet trophy.

It was a popular victory, a welcome evidence that attacking
football and intuitive genius still had their place in a footballing
world obsessed by 'work-rate' and (often) skill-less hard running.
Winning the tournament in 1966 England had conceded only
three goals, scored eleven. Four years later, the Brazilians had
triumphed by conceding seven goals and scoring nineteen.
Either England or West Germany – not to mention Uruguay –
might have made of the Final more than did the Italians. And it
remained true (as it may always remain true) that some of the
refereeing left much to be desired. But Ferenc Puskas, and many
other great stars of the past, would have approved. The football
of the Brazilians was many miles removed from the 'war' that
people had gloomily forecast as being the only result of international competition. Above all, the Brazilians made the thing
look enjoyable, had helped to restore that enthusiasm without
which sport in any form will wither away. More chants of 'samba',
and the spectacle of the greatest player of that, or any, generation
– Pelé – being raised aloft by delighted Brazilian fans.

1970 – Final Stages

Quarter-Finals

WEST GERMANY 3, ENGLAND 2 (0-1) (2-2) after extra
time. *Leon*

WEST GERMANY: Maier; Schnellinger, Vogts, Fichtel, Hottges
(Schulz); Beckenbauer, Overath, Seeler; Libuda (Grabowski),
Muller, Loehr.
ENGLAND: Bonetti (Chelsea); Newton (Everton); Cooper
(Leeds United); Mullery (Spurs), Labone (Everton), Moore

(West Ham United); Lee (Manchester City), Ball (Everton),
Hurst (West Ham United), Charlton (Manchester United)
[Bell (Manchester City)], Peters (Spurs) [Hunter (Leeds
United)].
SCORERS: Mullery, Peters for England; Beckenbauer, Seeler,
Muller for West Germany.

BRAZIL 4, PERU 2 (2-1). *Guadalajara*

BRAZIL: Felix; Carlos Alberto, Brito, Piazza, Marco Antonio;
Clodoaldo, Gerson (Paulo Cesar); Jairzinho (Roberto), Tostao,
Pelé, Rivelino.
PERU: Rubiños; Campos, Fernandez, Chumpitaz, Fuentes;
Mifflin, Challe; Baylon (Sotil), Perico Leon (Eladio Reyes),
Cubillas, Gallardo.
SCORERS: Rivelino, Tostao (2), Jairzinho for Brazil; Gallardo,
Cubillas for Peru.

ITALY 4, MEXICO 1 (1-1). *Toluca*

ITALY: Albertosi; Burgnich, Cera, Rosato, Facchetti; Bertini,
Mazzola (Rivera), De Sisti; Domenghini (Gori), Boninsegna,
Riva.
MEXICO: Calderon; Vantolra, Pena, Guzman, Perez; Gonzales
(Borja), Pulido, Munguia (Diaz); Valdivia, Fragoso, Padilla.
SCORERS: Domenghini, Riva (2), Rivera for Italy; Gonzales for
Mexico.

URUGUAY 1, RUSSIA 0 (0-0) after extra time. *Mexico*

URUGUAY: Mazurkiewicz; Ubinas, Ancheta, Matosas, Mujica;
Maneiro, Cortes, Montero Castillo; Cubilla, Fontes (Gomez),
Morales (Esparrago).
RUSSIA: Kavazashvili; Dzodzuashvili, Afonin, Khurtsilava
(Logofet), Chesternijev; Muntijan, Asatiani (Kiselev), Kapli-
chni; Evriuzhkinzin, Bychevetz, Khmelnitzki.
SCORER: Esparrago for Uruguay.

Semi-Finals

ITALY 4, WEST GERMANY 3 (1-0) (1-1) after extra time.
Mexico City

ITALY: Albertosi; Cera; Burgnich, Bertini, Rosato, (Poletti)
Facchetti; Domenghini, Mazzola (Rivera), De Sisti; Bonin-
segna, Riva.
WEST GERMANY: Maier; Schnellinger; Vogts, Schulz, Becken-
bauer, Patzke; Seeler, Overath; Grabowski, Muller, Loehr
(Libuda).
SCORERS: Boninsenga, Burgnich, Riva, Rivera, for Italy;
Schnellinger, Muller (2) for West Germany.

BRAZIL 3, URUGUAY 1 (1-1). *Guadalajara*

BRAZIL: Felix; Carlos Alberto, Brito, Piazza, Everaldo; Clodo-
aldo, Gerson; Jairzinho, Tostao, Pelé, Rivelino.
URUGUAY: Mazurkiewicz; Ubinas, Ancheta, Matosas, Mujica;
Montero Castillo, Cortes, Fontes; Cubilla, Maneiro (Esparrago),
Morales.
SCORERS: Cubilla for Uruguay; Clodoaldo, Jairzinho, Rivelino
for Brazil.

Third Place Match

WEST GERMANY 1, URUGUAY 0 (1-0). *Mexico City*
WEST GERMANY: Walter, Schnellinger (Lorenz); Patzke,
Fichtel, Weber, Vogts; Seeler, Overath; Libuda (Loehr),
Muller, Held.
URUGUAY: Mazurkiewicz; Ubinas, Ancheta, Matosas, Mujica;
Montero Castillo, Cortes, Fontes (Sandoval); Cubilla, Maneiro
(Esparrago), Morales.
SCORER: Overath for West Germany.

Final

BRAZIL 4, ITALY 1 (1-1). *Mexico City*

BRAZIL: Felix; Carlos Alberto, Brito, Piazza, Everaldo; Clodo-
aldo, Gerson; Jairzinho, Tostao, Pelé, Rivelino.
ITALY: Albertosi; Cera; Burgnich, Bertini, (Juliano), Rosato,
Facchetti; Domenghini, Mazzola, De Sisti; Boninsegna (Rivera),
Riva.
SCORERS: Pelé, Gerson, Jairzinho, Carlos Alberto for Brazil;
Boninsegna for Italy.

3 HOLLAND FINALISTS ON TWO OCCASIONS

Victorious West Germany – at last (1974)

Second in the tournament of 1966; third in that of 1970 West
Germany finally got their reward in the 1974 World Cup
finals. They had received a fillip two years previously when, with
Gunther Netzer at the top of his form as a play-maker in
midfield, they had won the 1972 edition of the European Nations
Championship; and they had received a recent bit of prompting
when a club side, Bayern Munich, had won the 1974 edition of
the European Champions' Cup

For the first time since 1950 the format would be changed with
the top two teams in each group not moving on to contest the
quarter-finals but to play in two further groups. The winners of
these would contest the Final, the teams who would finish second

would meet to decide the third and fourth places.

In 1970 it was teams from the Americas who had won four of
the eight places for the quarter-finals and had provided the most
convincing winners of any tournament to date, but four years
later the boot was very much on the European foot with West
Germany being followed home by Holland and Poland. The
Holland of Cruyff, of Neeskens, of Van Hanegem in fact could
stand comparison with the most commanding of the sides which
had won the World Cup for Brazil. And the measure of the
superiority shown by European sides was the fact that the only
occasion on which a South American team had a victory over a
European one was when Brazil defeated East Germany in a
match from the Second Round. In truth the South American
sides suffered most terribly from their lack of physical preparation – with Uruguay in particular exercising the most lethal form
of thuggery; especially when they met Holland in a game in
the First Round.

Brazil opened the tournament by playing very defensively
against Yugoslavia. True Pelé had chosen not to play; Gerson,
Tostao and Clodoaldo had all suffered vital injuries and the only
members of the 1970 side left were Rivelino and Jairzinho but the
great strength of the team on this occasion seemed to lie in its
defence with Leao proving a more than useful goalkeeper, with
Luis Pereira proving an excellent central defender and with the
blond fullback, Francisco Marinho, surging forward with some
useful runs down the left side of the field: 0–0 then with the
Yugoslavs being impressive in the second part of the game.
Maric had shown that he was a fine goalkeeper, Buljan made
several telling interceptions at the back and Acimovic had been
most intelligent in suggesting pathways for the attack.

Brazil's next game would also be goal-less – but on this
occasion against Scotland who had beaten Zaire 2–0 in their first
game in the Group. In the first twenty minutes the champions
from South America seemed set to tear Scotland apart with their
inventive football and skill at taking free-kicks; but gradually
Scotland came into the game strongly and as the game progressed
the authority of Billy Bremner in midfield became absolute.

David Hay became an increasingly important figure alongside him and both men saw scoring chances pass inches wide on the wrong side of the goalpost. With Holton and Buchan totally neutralising the potential threat from Jairzinho; with Lorimer and Morgan having fine games; with Bremner and Hay sealing up the middle of the field by their intelligent use of the ball – many people thought Scotland were desperately unfortunate not to gain a win. Yugoslavia demolished Zaire 9-0 on the same day, so Scotland went into the next game against Yugoslavia needing to win; or hoping against hope that Brazil would win by less than a two-goal margin against Zaire. With the two matches taking place at the same time matters looked promising at half-time, for Brazil had been unable to score more than once; and the Scotland-Yugoslavia game was still goal-less. But halfway through the second period a Rivelino left-footed shot screamed into the Zaire goal; and soon after Valdomiro added a third. Worse was to follow as Karasi, who had come on the field only minutes before as a substitute for the Yugoslavians, scored with a. header which left Scotland needing two goals in seven minutes. It was not to be, however, for although Jordan scored in the final minute of the game, Scotland were left rueing their failure to score against Brazil and the plain truth that they had taken matters far too easily against Zaire. They would have the small consolation of remaining the only team playing in the tournament to stay unbeaten and the fact that Bremner and McGrain would feature prominently in the lists of the best players who had been on duty in West Germany.

Group 1 saw the host nation being drawn against Australia, Chile and East Germany: the first occasion on which the two Germanies had played each other since the partition after the last war. Chile had come to the tournament by a curious route. They had been forced to play a deciding eliminator against Russia, had been there and drawn 0-0, then had been give a walk-over to the Finals proper when the Russians had refused to play the return match in Santiago – a refusal which had much more to do with political than sporting reasons, since Chile had recently experienced a right-wing coup! Despite some sinuous dribbling on

the part of Caszely, some vigorous defensive work by Figueroa
and some sharp bursts of counter-attacking by Ahumada, the
West Germans hung on to win by just a single goal. Chile next
held East Germany, who had beaten a gallant Australia 2–0, to a
1–1 draw. In their turn West Germany beat Australia 3–0 which,
of course, meant that when the two Germanies played their
'inaugural' match the home side were already qualified to play in
the Second Round; so it came as little surprise to find the East
defeating the West merely by the one goal – a defeat which meant
that West Germany would (be able to!) avoid the thrilling
Holland team for a further handful of matches.

In truth Holland had enthralled everybody in their opening
matches. Teams representing Dutch clubs had featured in five of
the previous six editions of the European Cup, and had been
victorious on four occasions; and the coach responsible for the
pressing football that had gained an enormous reputation all over
the world, Rinus Michels, had recently been called back to take
charge of the Holland squad. The team contained exciting
fullbacks in Suurbier and Krol, gifted players in the midfield in
Neeskens and Van Hanegem and in attack they possessed in
Johan Cruyff one of the two best players in the tournament (the
other being Franz Beckenbauer). Certainly their class was
immediately apparent in the first game they played, a 2–0 victory
against a crude and ruthless Uruguay. Uruguay played as though
they were totally deprived of skill and talent; three players were
cautioned, Julio Montero Castillo was sent off for aiming a series
of knee-high tackles, and only Mazurkiewicz in goal and Rocha
in midfield showed any type of form. A 1–1 draw against Bulgaria
and a 3–0 defeat by Sweden and it was small wonder that Roberto
Porta, the Uruguayan manager, stated just prior to the return of
the team to Montevideo, 'This is the worst football we have ever
played. It is a national disgrace.'

Sweden had proved to be one of the most interesting of teams
in the opening games. They began with two goal-less draws
against Bulgaria and Holland but in their 3–0 win over the
Uruguayans they had showed that they were coming into useful
form at just the right time. They possessed one of the better

goalkeepers in the tournament in Ronnie Hellstroem, had useful players in midfield in Grahn and Bo Larsson and in Edstroem were served by one of the most skilful of goalscorers. And the two teams to move on to the Second Round, therefore, were Sweden and Holland, who slaughtered Bulgaria 4-1 with two of their goals coming from penalties by Neeskens.

In Group IV we had a riveting start to the second half of the game between Italy and Haiti when the first goal came from . . . Haiti! In fact that score by Sanon was the first goal to have been let in by Dino Zoff for 1,143 minutes of international play. It set the football world wondering: were we in for as big an upset as England's defeat in 1950 at the hands of the United States or as Italy's defeat in 1966 at the hands of North Korea? No. Italy pulled themselves together and although the goalkeeper for Haiti, Francillon, made a series of superb saves, the Italians ran out 3-1 winners at the end of the game. A sour footnote to this, for a Haiti defender Ernest Jean-Joseph was found to have taken drugs before the match, was beaten up and sent home in disgrace on the orders of Jean-Claude Duvalier, son of 'Papa Doc'. R.I.P.?

On the same day Poland, the conquerors of England in the qualification group, made their first appearance in the competition when they faced Argentina – and fascinated everybody with the poise of their football. Many members of this team had taken part two years earlier when Poland had been Olympic champions; in Deyna they had one of the most intelligent and skilful of midfield players on view; in the young Zmuda and the tall, blond Gorgon they possessed a pair of effective central defenders; and in Lato and Szarmach they had players who could score smoothly. In fact both struck in the 3-2 win by Poland; and these two scored four goals in the 7-0 triumph over Haiti – with the prowess of Francillon ensuring that the defeat did not enter double figures as he made one crucial save after another. It was small wonder that in the following season he would come to West Germany to play his football as a mercenary.

On the same day Argentina and Italy played out an entertaining 1-1 draw. Despite the presence of 50,000 Italian supporters

in the crowd of just under 72,000, the Italians just could not put
things right. Although Mazzola played intelligently throughout
the game both Riva and Rivera were badly 'off song'; and a vital
mistake on the part of the Italian coach, Feruccio Valcarreggi,
made the game awkward for Italy when, as a marker for the small,
lively, Argentine winger Houseman, he appointed Capello – an
attacking midfield player! This move turned Capello into a
quasi-fullback; and although Valcarreggi understood his mistake
too late, the damage had already been done. Houseman it was
who scored for Argentina; and the only manner in which the
Italians could score their goal (which fortunately for them made
the game a draw) was to force the Argentine centreback,
Perfumo, to put the ball into his own net. So they went into their
next game against Poland requiring just a draw to pass through to
the next round.

Alas, it was not to be. Poland won 2-1 but in truth the Italians
were overwhelmed. Mazzola played effectively throughout,
Anastasi was incisive in the first-half and Facchetti resolute in the
second, but the Poland midfield of Deyna, Kasperczak and
Maszczyk was dominant throughout, with the first-named being
the best player on view as well as the scorer of one of the Polish goals.
With Argentina beating Haiti 4-1, with Babington continuing his
good run of form and despite the heroics of Francillon in the Haiti
goal, the Italians finished third in their qualifying group, behind
Argentina on goal difference. Small wonder that *La Squadra* found
itself being attacked as it left the stadium by its 'supporters'!

East Germany, West Germany, Yugoslavia, Brazil, Holland,
Sweden, Poland and Argentina therefore went through to the
Second Round. Holland, in their first game, set about the
unfortunate Argentina in the manner born, with Cruyff scoring
once in each half and with the whole team totally dominating the
game. The other goals in the 4-0 victory came from Rep and Krol
and, although Suurbier was forced to leave the field injured, the
Dutch were extremely fortunate in team selection throughout the championship, having comparatively few injuries, and
they were able to choose ten of their team for all seven of the
games.

In the same group Brazil defeated East Germany by just the single goal. In the 60th minute they were awarded a free-kick some ten metres outside the East German penalty area, Dirceu broke from the 'wall' at the last moment and allowed a cannonball of a shot from Rivelino to scream through. A fast-moving drive from Rivelino was the first score in their next game against Argentina – a game which Brazil won by 2-1, and the reply soon after by Brindisi was the first goal to be given away in the tournament by Brazil. A header by Jairzinho proved to be the eventual goal, and Brazil moved on to play the Dutch in their final game in the group; there they received a nice, sharp lesson in football skill, for although the introduction of Dirceu on the left side of the midfield had given them a far greater degree of penetration, they were still a team lacking in the highest of talents. In the crucial game their defenders chopped and hacked the Dutch from the outset, encouraging the retribution which their opponents were not slow to deliver. Ze Maria perpetrated a rugby tackle on Cruyff; Neeskens found himself being knocked cold by one of the centre-backs in Mario Marinho then being scythed down by the other, Luis Pereira. For his pains Pereira found himself being sent off. But the two goals in the first period of the second-half were worth waiting for: Neeskens played a free-kick to Cruyff on his right, dashed forward and struck the return over the head of the Brazilian goalkeeper, Leao. And the second was scored by Cruyff driving home a centre by Rensenbrink. It was a memorable day, indeed, for Dutch football which had seemed to say 'The King is Dead, Long Live the King'.

It came as no surprise to learn that the response after the game in Brazil was severe: coffins of the leading players were paraded in the streets and an effigy of Zagalo, the manager, was burnt.

The other group saw matches between West Germany and Yugoslavia, won by the Germans 2-0, and between Poland and Sweden won by the Poles by just the odd goal, scored by the man who would finish as the leading scorer in the tournament, Lato. In the first of these games West Germany for the first time in this tournament used Rainer Bonhof, whose skills with the ball and intelligent running into space gave a new dimension to the play of the European Nations Champions, so that the second half of the game should have seen more than the second goal scored by Gerd Muller. And most noticeable in the other game was the dribbling of Gadocha, the opportunism of Lato, the acrobatics of the goalkeeper Tomaszewski, and the organisation of Deyna. In fact, after losing this encounter it fell to the Swedes to tackle West Germany, a game which they lost 4-2, three of these goals being scored soon after half-time in a three-minute period.

The fortunes of the two teams were reversed at half-time, Sweden going in with a 1-0 lead; but West Germany came back strongly, with Bonhof in particular in glorious form on the right side of their midfield, scoring the second goal that put his side into the lead.

On the same day Poland beat Yugoslavia 2-1 with goals from Deyna and Lato; a score that was repeated three days later when Sweden beat the Yugoslavs but since neither side could hope to progress further, this game turned out to be packed with entertaining and spirited football, with both Maric and Hellstroem given many opportunities to show what excellent goalkeepers they were. (Indeed, many thought that they were the two most gifted goalkeepers in the entire tournament.) And this left the match between West Germany and Poland to decide which team would take part in the final.

West Germany won by a second-half goal by Gerd Muller, but many felt that the game should not have taken place when it did. A rainstorm had made the pitch unplayable, and although the West German authorities drew off as much water as they could and put the time of the match back, it could have been postponed until the following day. Tomaszewski saved a penalty from Holzenbein, but in the first-half Maier made an incredible double-save from Lato and Gadocha to put heart into the Germans. Beckenbauer was beginning to display authoritative form in defence, and the midfield of Bonhof, Hoeness and Overath gradually stood up to the Polish wiles of Deyna and Kaspercak.

Poland would have the small satisfaction of beating Brazil in the match to determine third and fourth places: a just reward for

having entertained so many people with their thrilling football
over the previous four weeks. The goal was from Lato, Poland
showing itself once more to be thoroughly more imaginative and
interesting; Brazil had a strong defence and midfield but a
pitifully inadequate attack. It was an uninspiring game.

But the Final, the following day, got off to an electric start
when Holland were awarded a penalty by the English referee,
Jack Taylor, within the first minute and before any West
German had touched the ball! 1–0 to Holland, and for
the following twenty-five minutes the Dutch arrogantly rolled
the ball about to each other, making pretty patterns, and
under no threat whatsoever from the West Germans, who were
entirely stunned. Then West Germany were awarded a penalty
of their own when Holzenbein was tripped inside the area by
Jansen, and when Gerd Muller gave West Germany a 2–1 lead
just before half-time the Dutch were really shaken. The crucial
issue in the match, however, was the man-to-man marking of
Cruyff by the West German fullback, Bertie Vogts. Cruyff was
undoubtedly the most gifted attacking player in the tournament,
possessing a footballing brain that was lightning fast, and all the
attributes of phenomenal players – lovely balance, glorious ball
control and an exceptional shot in either foot. With his being so
effectively shackled throughout the game, the effect on Holland,
in psychological as well as in physical terms, was crucial; and
after the West Germans had been awarded a penalty they played
with new spirit, Franz Beckenbauer very astutely marshalling his
forces in defence. With Rainer Bonhof spurring the midfield, and
Grabowski aiding Muller up front, and West Germany were able
to hang onto that first-half lead and take the tenth edition of the
World Cup.

It had been a real mixture of a tournament. Among the matters
that had been frowned upon some said that the new formula for
the tournament had led to much careless or plain bad football
which had seen the eventual champions beaten in an unimportant game from the First Round. But surely no game
should be described as being 'unimportant'? And then there had
been the fact that while Australia had battled bravely the other

two weaker teams, Zaire and Haiti, had conceded 28 goals
between them. Elementary arithmetic, here, for without those
games and goals you get 69 goals in 32 games which would be by
some measure the worst goals per game average. In addition
some nations – or rather the players of some nations – had taken
to demanding fees for giving interviews and vast sums for
succeeding in winning the title.

On the positive side, however, was the firmness and quality of
some of the refereeing and many, many moments of memorable
footballing skills. If the West German team that had won the
European Nations Championship two years previously had
played more fluid and imaginative football than the new holders
of the World Cup, some of the most memorable football had been
played by Sweden, by Poland and by Holland. Especially
Holland, who would be in the forefront of the competition four
years later.

1974 – Final Stages

Group A

	P	W	D	L	F	A
HOLLAND	3	3	0	0	8	0	6
BRAZIL	3	2	0	1	3	3	4
EAST GERMANY	3	0	1	2	1	4	1
ARGENTINA	3	0	1	2	2	7	1

Group B

WEST GERMANY	3	3	0	0	7	2	6
POLAND	3	2	0	1	3	2	4
SWEDEN	3	1	0	2	4	6	2
YUGOSLAVIA	3	0	0	3	2	6	0

Third Place Match played in Munich

POLAND 1, BRAZIL 0 (1-0) Lato for Poland

POLAND: Tomaszewski; Szymanowski, Gorgon, Musial; Kasperczak (Cmikiewicz), Deyna, Maszczyk; Lato, Szarmach (Kapka), Gadocha.

BRAZIL: Leao; Ze Maria, Alfredo, M. Marinho, F. Marinho; Paulo Cesar Carpeggiani, Rivelino, Ademir da Guia (Mirandinha); Valdomiro, Jairzinho, Dirceu.

Final played in Munich

WEST GERMANY 2, HOLLAND 1 (2-1) Breitner (pen.), Muller for West Germany and Neeskens (pen.) for Holland

WEST GERMANY: Maier; Vogts, Schwarzenbeck, Beckenbauer, Breitner; Bonhof, Hoeness, Overath; Grabowski, Muller, Holzenbein.

HOLLAND: Jongbloed; Suurbier, Rijsbergen (De Jong), Haan, Krol; Jansen, Neeskens, Van Hanegem; Rep, Cruyff, Rensenbrink (R. Van de Kerkhof)

Another Home Victory in Argentina (1978)

Never has a political background so affected a World Cup tournament. Before the military junta of General George Videla seized power in 1976, many had been extremely concerned that the 1978 edition of the World Cup had been given to Argentina; but after the coup fears were increased when thousands of people were tortured, imprisoned without trial or simply 'disappeared', never to be heard of again. The junta set up a new body, the Ente Autarquico Mundial to make sure that all preparations for the tournament – including the construction of three new stadia and the remodelling of three others – would be carried out in time. And there can be little doubt that, without the setting up of the EAM and the hard work done by this body, the tournament would probably have been relocated to Brazil, Mexico or Spain. And the corollary of that, of course, was that there was that much more extra pressure on Argentina to win!

The presence of great players obviously helps the prestige of a tournament: and, sadly, the two heroes of the 1974 World Cup chose not to take part. Franz Beckenbauer had, fifteen months previously, signed for New York Cosmos for $2,500,000 and Johan Cruyff absolutely refused to take part, despite huge offers. These two were not the only absentees. West Germany had to compete without the talents of Gerd Muller, Wolfgang Overath, Paul Breitner, Uli Hoeness and Jurgen Grabowski; and Wim van Hanegem dropped out at the last moment after being informed that he could not count on a regular place in the side. The host country, Argentina, had lost several players from her 1974 side who had moved to play in Europe such as Kempes, Brindisi, Carnevali, Wolff and Heredia, who were now in Spain, and Babington who had moved to West Germany. When it came down to it Cesar-Luis Menotti, nick-named El Flaco (the Thin One) expressed interest in only Kempes, Wolff and Oswaldo Piazza playing at centre-back for the French club of St Etienne. In the event, Wolff could not be released by Real Madrid and the family of Piazza were involved in a road accident, so Kempes was the only man to join the squad.

Scotland were favoured by many. They had had a successful tour of South America in 1977, and in their qualifying group had eliminated the 1976 winners of the European Championship, Czechoslovakia. Even though their final win in the qualifying round had been in part thanks to a penalty that wasn't in their match away against Wales, euphoria was high. WE'RE ON OUR WAY TO RIO, trumpeted a headline in a Scottish daily paper with a neat disregard for geography. 'Of course we'll win the World Cup. If I say that it saves you from asking me again,' said the ebullient Scottish manager Ally Macleod, who favoured Hungary were Scotland not to succeed in their mission! (Hungary joined Mexico as being the only two countries not to win any point whatsoever.) He paid a visit to Cordoba in the January of 1978 and was delighted with the accommodation – so the feedback to Scotland's fans was just what they required. But the few realists in their camp had other evidence. Danny McGrain would be ruled out of this World Cup through injury; Gordon McQueen, the first-choice stopper, would receive an injury only a fortnight before the tournament that would rule him out; and much to the surprise of everyone, Andy Gray, the young central striker who was on top form, would not make the selection.

Brazil were favourites to do well, perhaps even to win the tournament. They had dismissed Oswaldo Brandao a year previously and had appointed in his place a young army captain, Claudio Coutinho, who was attempting to 'Europeanise' the Brazilian game by placing the emphasis on stamina and covering each blade of grass on the pitch. A far cry indeed from those days of Pelé, Gerson and Tostao. Coutinho had compounded his strategy by not selecting Francisco Marinho, who had been one of the most-admired fullbacks in the previous tournament as well as that wayward forward, Paulo Cesar.

Italy, the conquerors of the qualifying group above England – and the only team to qualify on goal difference – were given scant chance of success. The chief play-maker to the team, Giancarlo Antognoni, had been having a desperate season trying to prevent his club side of Fiorentia from being relegated; and for some months had suffered a strain to his right ankle which had required a complete rest. In addition, his wife had a miscarriage only a few days prior to Italy's first game against France. Giacinto Facchetti, the sweeper, was ruled out of football altogether, having been on the receiving end of a tackle from Romeo Benetti. The team had recently recruited a young fullback, Cabrini, who was strong in the tackle and eager to set up counter-attacks; at their training camp, spent just outside Buenos Aires, Enzo Bearzot, the Italian manager, decided that the time had come to be brave and to play Paolo Rossi the young, adroit and courageous forward who had just finished the season in Italy as the chief scorer. With Marco Tardelli settling firmly into his role as a defensive player in midfield Bearzot hoped, above all, to encourage the Italian team to play more open

football, completely throw off those defensive shackles which
were set firm in the Italian club game and attempt to play more
freely. He would have his wish much sooner than he could have
expected!

It came after thirty-eight seconds of play in the first of Italy's
games in Group I when Didier Six collected a glorious through
pass from the midfield, raced down the left touchline and crossed
the ball into the centre for Bernard Lacombe to out-jump the
Italian defence and head a simple goal. Thunder-struck the
Italians simply knew that they had then to attack and take the
game into the French half, to stand any chance of gaining a
victory and driven on by the experience of Romeo Benetti, by the
fact that Tardelli carried out a masterly shackling job on Michel
Platini, by the smooth manner in which Bettega and Rossi
formed a partnership in the attack, Italy won the game 2-1. On
the same day Argentina had had a 2-1 win over Hungary with two
Hungarians, Nyilasi and Toroscik, being sent off for committing
ugly fouls at the end of the game. Yet the atmosphere in the River
Plate stadium was sour from the start, with a snowstorm of
Argentinian favours thrown onto the pitch as the teams came
out; tension throughout that could have been cut with a knife.

Four days later Italy had little difficulty in defeating a depleted
Hungarian team 3-1 but one of the best matches of the
tournament was to take place that same evening in Buenos Aires
when Argentina defeated a gallant France by a 2-1 scoreline. It
was truly an enthralling spectacle, every minute packed with
good football – and atrocious refereeing decisions on the part of
the Swiss officals; Jean Dubach, 'gave' Argentina a penalty
when the accomplished black sweeper Marius Tresor landed on
the ball while challenging Luque in the penalty area and was
adjudged to have handled it intentionally. And this in injury
time! It was a monstrous decision compounding the fact that the
referee had failed to award France a penalty of their own when
Six was pulled down in the penalty area. And the same player
should have scored, following a glorious run by Platini, but shot
wide when he had only the goalkeeper to beat. Lucky, lucky
Argentina.

Thus when Argentina met Italy again (following their drawn game in the 1974 tournament) both sides had already qualified for the Second Round. The match was, however, still important, as Argentina very much wished to stay in Buenos Aires and not have to travel to Rosario, over 300 kilometres to the north-east of the capital: which would be their fate if they failed to secure a victory. There would be no nonsense on this occasion about the refereeing for the choice had fallen to Abraham Klein who made it clear from the first that he would not 'play to the gallery'. With the Italians knowing that a draw would suit them – falling back on defensive man-to-man marking and making sudden breaks from defence into attack – the only goal of the game came in the sixty-seventh minute when, after an interchange of passes between Antognoni and Rossi, the latter slid a perfectly placed pass through to Bettega, who screwed his shot past Fillol, the commanding goalkeeper for Argentina. But although it was Bettega who won most of the glory, it should be pointed out that both Benetti and Causio ran their hearts out in midfield, and Gentile (called in as stopper after Cuccureddu had replaced the injured Bellugi) completely marked Kempes out of the game. And in the afternoon of the same day France received some reward when they defeated Hungary 3–1. A curious event happened before the game when France were asked to change their strip because television viewers with black and white sets found it hard to differentiate between the blue of France and the red of Hungary. A sure sign, this, of interests other than simple footballing ones being considered! Even though France were forced to leave the tournament after this win, they made a tournament record that year by being the only country playing to have used all twenty-two of their permitted players, with Marius Tresor the only man to have played in all 270 minutes of their games.

Group II saw West Germany play Poland play Mexico play Tunisia: the easiest of all the four groups. Sadly, it got off to a goal-less draw between West Germany and Poland – the fourth occasion in succession that the opening game in the tournament has been something of a 'goal-less grimmie'. Deyna was the man of the match directing operations in the midfield with skill and intelligence, and several famous faces from the Polish triumph of four years earlier were there: Gorgon and Zmuda in the middle of the defence and Lato and Szarmach in the attack. Also there was Wlodzimierz Lubanski, who had been put out of the game entirely for two years with an injury he had received in June 1973 when England had played Poland in Warsaw. Was this draw inevitable? Many people thought so, with both teams ensuring a place for themselves in the last eight.

The following day Tunisia amazed many people by defeating Mexico 3-1. Like many of the unknown teams in the past they possessed a player of absolute class a slim character in their midfield, Dhiab Tarak, who laid on all three goals for the African side – all scored in the second half, after Mexico had scored from a penalty just before half-time. This was a real test of character, and the group table at the end of the day would show Tunisia standing proudly above West Germany, Poland, and Mexico who had put on a pathetic display. Four days later Tunisia proved their worth against an altogether stronger team by holding Poland to a 1-0 win, totally dominating the second half and being most unfortunate not to gain a draw. Meanwhile Mexico was proving itself the weakest team in the competition by losing 6-0 to West Germany. And as if to add insult to injury, Tunisia next held West Germany to a goal-less draw while Poland beat Mexico 3-1, although Tomaszewski in their goal was called upon to save some five close shots from his opponents.

If the real heroes of the first two groups had been teams which would take no further part in the competition the games from the third group seemed more concerned with watching Brazil – the 9-4 favourites before the competition started – try to beat itself and not qualify for the Second Round. It was an unhappy ship. Rivelino was overweight and rebellious; Coutinho had fallen out with Zico, another of the stars; and it was as well that Amaral and Oscar played magnificently at the heart of the defence so that Brazil were the only team playing in this tournament to remain unbeaten, and that Batista and Cerezo produced play of the first order in midfield. They were held to a 1-1 draw by Sweden in the

opening game; and then drew 0-0 with Spain in the game which
they surely would have lost had not Cardenosa missed a
marvellous chance when right in front of the goal. In their third
game, however, they beat Austria 1-0. But Austria had already
qualified, thanks to two wins against Spain (2-1) and Sweden (1-
0) which left these two to play each other and see which team
would go through if Brazil slipped up. Spain won this affair 1-0 –
but they must have been somewhat forlorn to leave the
competition after having showed the most marvellous spirit in
defeating Rumania and Yugoslavia in their qualifying games.

Group IV saw Scotland drawn against Iran, Peru and
Holland; a draw which Ally Macleod, the Scottish manager, said
he 'wanted'. 'That leaves us to go through to the last eight with
Holland and after that the players won't need any motivating.'
We were never to find out, because although Scotland took an
early lead against Peru and completely dominated the first period
of the first half, things began to go sadly wrong. Cubillas,
Munante and Oblitas at last decided to run at the Scottish
defence and gradually started to drive it wild with a succession of
one-twos. Finally, the inevitable happened, and in the forty-
second minute Peru finally scored through Cueto. A disastrous
moment at which to give away a goal. Worse was to follow,
however, in the sixty-fourth minute, when Scotland were
awarded a penalty after Rioch was brought down by Cubillas.
Masson took the kick but it was a truly feeble effort which
Quiroga, in the Peruvian goal, found no trouble in saving. That
was Scotland's last chance, for Peru totally dominated the last 25
minutes of the game. Cubillas scored twice – and Scotland had a
bitter postscript when Willie Johnston their wing-forward, was
found to have taken 'pep' pills. So morale for the next match,
against Iran, couldn't have been lower.

Maybe that excuse could be used profitably, because the
match was one of the very worst there has ever been in the history
of the World Cup. Surely Scotland have never played such bad
football? The result was a 1-1 draw, with Scotland's score
coming from an own goal by Eskandarjan; one of the best
Scottish players, Martin Buchan was kicked in the face by the

man whose role at fullback he had taken in the first match, Willie
Donachie; and it could so easily have been another traumatic
defeat had not Ghasimpour shot straight at Rough when put
through in the first half. No wonder the hundreds of Scottish
supporters, who had travelled over 9,000 kilometres to
Argentina, began to wail with fury; no wonder that restaurants in
Glasgow which in former times had used the name of the
Scotland manager in their advertising started to put up signs
which read, 'Ally MacLeod does NOT eat here'!

Holland had shown how it could be done by beating Iran 3-0
and when it became the turn of Peru they won 4-1; so when these
two sides met it came as no surprise to find them playing very
cagily, settling for a 0-0 draw.

Experts often point out that Scotland play terribly against
poor teams, handsomely against the good ones. And so it proved
when Scotland played Holland in their final match. The team
selection was put right at long last, with Souness being played in
midfield and proving that he was exactly the right link to get the
best out of Dalglish up front. In fact it was Dalglish who volleyed
Scotland's equaliser ten minutes after Rensenbrink had given
Holland a lead in the thirty-fourth minute with a penalty: the
1000th goal in the history of the World Cup. Scotland got their
retribution early in the second half when Gemmill scored a
penalty after Krol was adjudged to have fouled Souness, and in
the sixty-eighth minute the same player scored what was
admitted by some to be the best goal of this World Cup, when he
jinked his way through the Dutch defence to score with a hard
shot from close range. The Scottish supporters had a bare four
minutes of wishful thinking about their appearance in the Second
Round before Rep laid their wish to rest, scoring with a
screaming shot from 23 metres.

What had gone wrong with Scotland and their hopes? Partly
the blame lay in the arrogance with which Scotland had gone to
Argentina, having done far too little homework as to the
strengths and weaknesses of their opponents; partly it lay in team
selection – in the loyalty to Rioch and Masson, who had been
dropped by their club sides, in the under-use of Souness; partly

it lay in the accommodation which left the players very bored
when not depressed; and partly with the players themselves –
many of whom simply did not realise how much they had let
down their supporters. But these supporters themselves were to
blame. 'Bring on the English' they roared when, at one stage in
the game against Holland they seemed to be in with a chance of
reaching the last eight.

Group A in the Second Round consisted of Italy, West
Germany, Austria and Holland; Group B of Argentina, Poland,
Brazil and Peru. Of these, Italy was the only country to have
won all its games in the early stages and those wins had been
achieved in what many people thought had been the most
difficult group, and by a new formula of play: Enzo Bearzot had
dragged his players away from the negativity induced by
catenaccio (man-to-man marking plus a sweeper) and introduc-
ing the Total Football which had been played by Holland in
the previous World Cup and the West German team in
1972.

In their first game in the Second Round Italy played West
Germany, and optimists hoped for an encounter as entertaining
as that when they had last met in a World Cup, the 4-3 victory by
Italy in a semi-final in 1970. No chance of that on this occasion:
Italy were now regarded as an attacking team and from the first
moment West Germany settled down to play a form of *catenaccio*
with Rumenigge and Holzenbein on the wings being drawn back
to play in midfield and Klaus Fischer left alone in the attack. 0-0
the result (the third goal-less draw out of West Germany's four
games to date), but Bettega missed two chances from close
distance – and the Italian triumphal march had been stopped.

On the same day Holland had a most uplifting 5-1 victory over
Austria in Cordoba. The Dutch players showed fresh zest on
being away at last from the heights of Mendoza; Holland were
able to call upon some talented substitutes in Pieter Wildschut
and Erny Brandts, the 22-year-old centre-back; and the injury to
Neeskens had given a chance to Arie Haan. Johnny Rep scored
two of the goals and Robbie Rensenbrink scored from a penalty
and showed that he was coming back into form. A most

significant win, this, in psychological terms, as well as being most disheartening for the other teams.

Four days later Holland played West Germany at Cordoba, with the Dutch hyper-keen to reverse the result of the previous World Cup Final. They began their mission miserably, going down after only three minutes to a tap-in by Abramczik, when a thundering free-kick by Bonhof had only been parried by Schrivers, but when they equalised in the twenty-sixth minute it was with a truly memorable shot on the part of Haan, who let fly from roughly 25 metres out. Maier never even touched the ball. It was the first occasion in which he had been beaten in 475 minutes of play in World Cup games: a new record. West Germany, however, were playing with considerably more character than they had shown in their game against Italy, and took the lead again in the seventieth minute when Dieter Muller headed in a centre; it was only after Holland had taken off Wildschut and substituted that angular forward, Dirk Nanninga, that they were able to get a draw from the game. He it was who helped Rene Van der Kerkhof slice in from the left and put the ball past Maier from a narrow distance.

On the same day in Buenos Aires Italy beat Austria 1-0, thanks to a goal from Rossi scored in the thirteenth minute – after which the team just fell back on defence. Austria showed very little wit or imagination in their play (in fact that goal of Rossi's had followed an unwise back pass from a fullback), and Krankl spent much of the game being the lone ranger of the attack. He it was who scored the decisive goal three days later when Austria beat West Germany 3-2 after volleying the Austrian second goal. A very sad way for Helmut Schön to retire as manager of the West German team: first, third and second in the preceeding editions of the tournament. On the same day Holland came to play Italy in Buenos Aires. Thanks to their 5-1 victory over Austria they knew that all they had to do was to gain a draw. But in the first ten minutes Italy could have scored twice, and in fact they took the lead in the nineteenth minute when Brandts skimmed the ball past Schrivers into the goal – in an attempt to stop Bettega from scoring. As well as giving away an own goal, he damaged the right

knee of the goalkeeper, who had to be substituted soon after by
Jan Jongbloed, the goalkeeper from the 1974 side who, while still
'cold' made two astonishing saves from Rossi and Benetti. Then
the wrestling began: Benetti kicked Haan and fouled
Rensenbrink, and in retribution Haan booted Zaccarelli and Rep
flattened Benetti. By half-time the names of Rep and Benetti
were in the book and it was then that Bearzot made the grave
mistake of taking off Franco Causio – who had played skilfully
down the right wing – and putting on Claudio Sala. The Italian
rhythm went and soon after Brandts atoned for his own goal by
swinging his right-foot at the ball while surrounded by Italian
players and driving the ball through to score; and in the seventy-
seventh minute there came once more one of those thunderous
shots from Haan from 32 metres out, which nearly removed the
back of the net. Two minutes later Italy substituted Graziani for
Benetti in an attempt to score twice in the remaining minutes of
the game, but to no avail; and the cruel spate of fouling continued
with Haan himself and Cabrini and Tardelli being booked.
Holland were through to the Final.

In Group B Brazil at last began to play in the manner hoped
for by all their supporters. Away from the difficult playing
surface at Mar Del Plata, their first match was at Mendoza,
where they beat Peru 3-0 thanks to two goals from Dirceu, one of
these being from a free kick which swung inwards at the last
moment to leave Quiroga totally helpless. Zico came on as
substitute in the seventieth minute and scored from a penalty
soon after.

That evening Argentina beat Poland 2–0, thanks largely to
a skilful display by Mario Kempes who scored both goals
in the fifteenth and seventieth minutes, and rescued another by
making a spectacular save off the goal-line after Fillol had been
beaten. The penalty was taken by Deyna playing in his
hundredth international, but his weak shot was saved – and
Poland's last chance went. Although in the first half they had
played very well, with Boniek and Adam Nawalka outstanding
and although a shot from Lato hit the side-netting early in the
second half, it became increasingly one-way traffic, with

Argentina spurred on by the baying of the crowds, who seemed much more intense at Rosario than they had been in the larger stadium at Buenos Aires. A real 'pressure-cooker' of a ground.

You think that games between England and Scotland have an electric atmosphere? Forget it. When Argentina play Brazil hatred is a factor that is present even before the ball has been kicked. Four players were booked; others 'left their feet' in many instances showing theirs studs and Ricardo Villa, who had come on for Ardiles after half-time, was extremely fortunate not to be sent off after committing an over-the-ball foul on Batista, the Brazilian midfield player. It was a truly forgettable goal-less draw with little football managing to survive all the spitefulness.

In the afternoon of the same day Poland had beaten Peru 1-0 but truly the score could have been in double figures. Why wasn't it? Thanks to that remarkable goalkeeper, Ramon Quiroga, who made amazing saves all through the game and in the final minutes advanced beyond the halfway line in order to break up the Polish attacks. Truly he deserved the nickname of 'El Loco'! The goal for Poland was scored by Szarmach, the woodwork was hit on two occasions and this feeble effort on the part of Peru can only have served to make all Scotsmen round the world feel most distressed by the memory of Scotland's weak displays.

The final day of this Round saw Brazil beat Poland 3-1. But rather it might be put the other way round because the Polish finishing was truly terrible. Both Lato and Szarmach seemed to have lost that vital edge of speed and thought which had made them so successful four years earlier, and although Leao was at the top of his form it is true to say that he absolutely had to be, because Poland's midfield players played with great authority. The first of Brazil's goals came from a swerving free kick of great power struck by Nelinho and the other two from Roberto. In that evening Argentina beat Peru. Why was the game started three-quarters of an hour after the game between Brazil and Poland had actually finished? Because of 'home' advantage; the argument being that Argentina should play all their games in the evening so that the crowds could attend without disrupting their work.

Ridiculous. Be that as it may, Argentina knew that the game had to be won by a clear four goals in order to give her a place in the Final. People will always see this game as being a 'fix', but the fact is that poor Peru were just overrun in the second half, after going in 2-0 down at half-time. In fact they could have scored twice themselves in the first half, when Munante and Oblitas both went near with chances. Kempes and Luque scored twice, with the other goals being scored by Tarantini and Houseman (a much less effective player than he had been in 1974). So it was Argentina versus Holland in the Final.

The day before we saw the match between Brazil and Italy to decide third and fourth places. Both teams possessed supporters and experts who thought that they were the best teams in the competition. Brazil had yet to lose a game, while the Italians, in addition to having beaten Argentina, felt that they had played the best football of the tournament. But, as against Holland, Italy allowed itself to be overtaken after Causio had scored a goal in the thirty-eighth minute. First Nelinho shot powerfully from the right corner and the ball swerved *inwards* to defeat Zoff, and the winning goal came from Dirceu, who swung in a fierce shot from just outside the penalty area. So Brazil retained their record of remaining unbeaten; however they could be considered unfortunate in two respects at least – that of playing their first round matches at Mar Del Plata on pitches that cut up horribly and of having Argentina play their last game after their own had finished.

Nor did it stop there, for before the Final had begun Holland's players came out onto the field five minutes before the home team, who instantly added to that piece of gamesmanship by objecting to the cast that was being worn by Rene Van der Kerkhof on his right wrist. He had suffered the injury in the first game of the tournament but none of the succeeding five opponents of the Dutch had objected! Eventually he was allowed to keep it on with a covering of bandage, but the psychological damage had been done. It was small wonder Holland began to play in a distressed and ugly mood. In addition, they had two further causes for worry: some most feeble refereeing by Sergio Gonella and the fact that Mario Kempès was in the most splendid form. For a long period the Argentina defence made mistake after mistake with Fillol making two superb saves from Rep and Rensenbrink and then suddenly, in the thirty-seventh minute, Argentina took the lead: Ardiles to Luque to Kempès who slid the ball into the goal, underneath the advancing Jongbloed.

In the first period of the second half each side made two substitutions: Nanninga for Rep, Larrosa for Ardiles, Suurbier for Jansen and Houseman for Ortiz. And it was the first-named of these who headed in a centre from the right in the eighty-first minute. Holland pressed forward even more aggressively and in the eighty-ninth minute Rensenbrink hit a post. Extra time, therefore; the first occasion in a Final since 1966 when another host country, England, had beaten the redoubtable West Germans. And it was during this period when Mario Kempès really came into his own, playing with all the skill, all the speed and all the composure that he knew. Bertoni put him through to score the goal that made him the highest scorer in the competition (although he hadn't scored at all in the first round): in the hundred-and-fourth minute when he struck in a rebound from his original shot; and ten minutes later he was able to play a one-two with Bertoni after which the winger scored. The host team had won for the second time in succession and Holland had had the chagrin of twice being defeated finalists.

102 goals had been scored, much good and entertaining football had been played; there had been thunderous goals from Haan, Rep, Cubillas and Luque, and clever ones from Dirceu, Gemmill, Schachner; there had been much intelligent running with the ball; a fair proportion of the refereeing had been wayward or weak and there had been some incredibly poor decisions – decisions which could have caused changes in some results. But overall the tournament was immensely better than one had dared to hope for and if the number of outstanding individuals was diminished then the manner in which teamwork had improved since the last tournament was most marked.

The final word, however, must be cautionary. Pressures on teams and their managers were far too intense and, with the idea of playing the first section of games in groups, we have the situation in which both the last two winners of the tournament have been beaten before they have ever reached the Final (West Germany by East Germany in 1974 and Argentina by Italy in 1978). With the next tournament being expanded to include twenty-four teams, the number of unimportant matches, the amount of bad and boring football, and mistakes by referees will simply rise, and all the prestige of the World Cup will sharply fall.

1978 Final Stages

Group A

HOLLAND	3	2	1	0	9	4	5
ITALY	3	1	1	1	2	2	3
WEST GERMANY	3	0	2	1	4	5	2
AUSTRIA	3	1	0	2	4	8	2

Group B

ARGENTINA	3	2	1	0	8	0	5
BRAZIL	3	2	1	0	6	1	5
POLAND	3	1	0	2	2	5	2
PERU	3	0	0	3	0	10	0

Third Place Match played in Buenos Aires

BRAZIL 2, ITALY 1 (0-1) Nelinho, Dirceu for Brazil, Causio for Italy

BRAZIL: Leao; Nelinho, Oscar, Amaral, Neto; Cerezo (Rivelino), Batista, Dirceu; Gil (Reinaldo), Mendonca, Roberto
ITALY: Zoff; Cuccureddu, Gentile, Scirea, Cabrini; Maldera, Antognoni (Sala C.), Sala P.; Causio, Rossi, Bettega

Final played in Buenos Aires

ARGENTINA 3, HOLLAND 1 (1-0) (1-1) Kempès (2), Bertoni for Argentina, Nanninga for Holland

ARGENTINA: Fillol; Olguin, Galvan, Passarella, Tarantini; Ardiles (Darrosa), Gallego, Kempès; Bertoni, Luque, Ortiz (Houseman)
HOLLAND: Jongbloed; Poortvliet, Brandts, Krol, Jansen (Suurbier); Haan, Neeskens, Van der Kerkhof W.; Rep (Nanninga), Rensenbrink, Van der Kerkhof R.

4 SOME STATISTICS

Number of Entries

1930 in Uruguay – 13
1934 in Italy – 32
1938 in France – 36
1950 in Brazil – 33
1954 in Switzerland – 38
1958 in Sweden – 51
1962 in Chile – 56
1966 in England – 53
1970 in Mexico – 70
1974 in West Germany – 93
1978 in Argentina – 105

Attendances at Final Matches

1930 at Montevideo – 90,000   URUGUAY 4 ARGENTINA 2
1934 at Rome – 50,000   ITALY 2 CZECHOSLOVAKIA 1
                                            (after extra time)
1938 at Paris – 45,000   ITALY 4 HUNGARY 2
1950 at Rio de Janeiro – 199,850   URUGUAY 2 BRAZIL 1
1954 at Berne – 60,000   WEST GERMANY 3 HUNGARY 2
1958 at Stockholm – 49,737   BRAZIL 5 SWEDEN 2
1962 at Santiago – 68,679   BRAZIL 3 CZECHOSLOVAKIA 1
1966 at London – 93,802   ENGLAND 4 WEST GERMANY 2
                                            (after extra time)
1970 at Mexico City – 107,412   BRAZIL 4 ITALY 1
1974 at Munich – 77,833   WEST GERMANY 2 HOLLAND 1
1978 at Buenos Aires – 77,000   ARGENTINA 3 HOLLAND 1
                                            (after extra time)

Pelé and Bobby Moore exchange shirts after Brazil had beaten England 1-0 in the 1970 World Cup.

Francis Lee busy in action during the Quarter-final game in the 1970 World Cup which England lost 2-3 in extra time after having led 2-0. Those watching are Brian Labone, Klaus Fichtel, Franz Beckenbauer, Sepp Maier, Uwe Seeler and Berti Vogts.

Gerd Muller scores West Germany's third goal in the Semi-final against Italy who eventually won 4-3. Gianni Rivera, Angelo Domenghini, Enrico Albertosi and Tarcisio Burgnich are the watching Italian players.

Brazil's Tostao attempting to negotiate a path past the Italians Roberto Rosato and Mario Bertini (r) during the 1970 Final which Brazil won 4-1.

The face of Billy Bremner tells the story as he watches his shot skimming just past on the wrong side of the Brazilian goal. Leao is the beaten goalkeeper, Hay and Piazza the other players.

Joe Jordan fires a shot past Josip Katalinski and the goalkeeper, Enver Mario, to ensure that Scotland achieve a 1-1 draw with Yugoslavia that makes them the only side to remain unbeaten in the 1974 World Cup.

Ronnie Hellström leaps up to catch the ball and prevent Johan Cruyff from scoring in the Sweden-Holland match during the 1974 tournament. The other Swedish defender is Staffan Tapper.

Roberto Rivelino attempting to surge past two Dutch defenders during the game between Holland and Brazil in the 1974 World Cup, which the former won 2-0.

Gregorz Lato and goalkeeper Jan Tomaszewski of Poland after the match in which Poland beat Brazil 1-0 to achieve Third Place in the 1974 World Cup.

Johan Neeskens scores the penalty, which was given in the first minute of the 1974 Final between West Germany and Holland. The German goalkeeper is Sepp Maier.

Bernard Lacombe heads the ball to score the only goal for France after only 38 seconds in the 1-2 defeat by Italy in the 1978 World Cup. The Italian defenders are Antonio Cabrini (l) and Mauro Bellugi (r).

Hungary's goalkeeper, Ferenc Mezaros, on the ground after Paolo Rossi has scored the first Italian goal in the Italy-Hungary match during the 1978 World Cup, which Italy won 3-1.

Joe Jordan (9) and Kenny Dalglish embrace after the latter has scored the first Scotland goal in the 3-2 defeat of Holland in the 1978 World Cup.

Roberto Bettega scores the single goal of the game in which Italy inflicted a defeat on Argentina.

Nelinho of Brazil bends a free kick round the Polish defensive wall to score the first goal when the two countries met again in the 1978 World Cup.

Daniel Bertoni races away after scoring Argentina's last goal in the 3-1 victory over Holland in the 1978 Final. The other players are Mario Kempes, Leopoldo Luque and the beaten goalkeeper is Jan Jongbloed, who is appealing for offside.

Analysis of the winning teams in the World Cup

	P	W	D	L	F	A
1930 URUGUAY	4	4	0	0	15	3

15 players used. Ballesteros, Nasazzi, Cea, Andrade (J), Fernandez, Gestido, Iriarte 4 apps. each; Dorado, Mascheroni, Scarone 3 each; Castro, Anselmo 2 each; Tejera, Petrone, Urdinaran 1 each.

	P	W	D	L	F	A
1934 ITALY	5	4	1	0	12	3

17 players used. Combi, Allemandi, Monti, Meazza, Orsi 5 each; Monzeglio, Bertolini, Schiavio, Ferrari, Guiata 4 each; Ferraris IV 3; Pizziolo 2; Rosetta, Guarisi, Castellazzi, Borel, Demaris 1 each.

	P	W	D	L	F	A
1938 ITALY	4	4	0	0	11	5

14 players used. Olivieri, Rava, Serantoni, Andreolo, Locatelli, Meazza, Piolo, Ferrari 4 each; Foni, Biavati, Colaussi 3 each; Monzeglio, Pasinati, Ferraris 1 each.

	P	W	D	L	F	A
1950 URUGUAY	4	3	1	0	15	5

14 players used. Gonzales M., Tejera, Valera, Andrade R., Ghiggia, Perez, Miguez, Schiaffino 4 each; Maspoli, Vidal 3 each; Gonzales W., Gambetta 2 each; Paz, Moran 1 each.

	P	W	D	L	F	A
1954 WEST GERMANY	6	5	0	1	25	14

18 players used. Eckel, Walter F. 6 each; Turek, Kohlmeyer, Posipal, Mai, Morlock, Walter O., Schafer 5 each; Liebrich, Rahn 4 each; Laband 3; Klodt, Bauer 2 each; Mebus, Herrmann, Kwaitowski, Pfaff 1 each.

	P	W	D	L	F	A
1958 BRAZIL	6	5	1	0	16	4

16 players used. Gilmar, Nilton Santos, Bellini, Orlando, Didi, Zagalo 6 each; De Sordi 5; Vava, Zito, Garrincha, Pele 4 each; Mazzola 3; Dino, Joel 2 each; Djalma Santos, Dida 1 each.

	P	W	D	L	F	A
1962 BRAZIL	6	5	1	0	14	5

12 players used (the lowest number by any Winner). Gilmar,
Santos D., Santos N., Zozimo, Mauro, Zito, Didi, Vava,
Garrincha, Zagalo 6 each; Amarildo 4; Pele 2.

	P	W	D	L	F	A
1966 ENGLAND	6	5	1	0	14	3

15 players used. Banks, Cohen, Wilson, Stiles, Charlton J.,
Moore, Hunt, Charlton R. 6 each; Peters 5; Ball 4; Greaves,
Hurst 3 each; Paine, Callaghan, Connelly 1 each.

	P	W	D	L	F	A
1970 BRAZIL	6	6	0	0	19	7

16 players used. Felix, Carlos Alberto, Piazza, Brito, Clodoaldo,
Jairzinho, Pele, Tostao 6 each; Everaldo, Rivelino 5 each;
Gerson 4; Paulo Cesar 2 + 2 subs; Marco Antonia 1 + 1 sub;
Roberto 2 subs; Fontana 1; Edu 1 sub.

	P	W	D	L	F	A
1974 WEST GERMANY	7	6	0	1	13	4

18 players used. Maier, Vogts, Breitner, Schwarzenbeck,
Beckenbauer, Muller, Overath 7 each; Hoeness 6 + 1 sub;
Grabowski 5 + 1 sub; Bonhof 4; Holzenbein 4 + 2 subs; Cullman
3; Heynckes, Herzog 2 each; Flohe 1 + 2 subs; Wimmer 1 + 1 sub;
Netzer, Hottges 1 sub each.

	P	W	D	L	F	A
1978 ARGENTINA	7	5	1	1	15	4

17 players used. Fillol, Galvan L., Olguin, Passarella,
Tarantini, Gallego, Kempes 7 each; Ardiles 6; Bertoni 5 + 1
sub; Ortiz 4 + 2 subs; Luque 5; Houseman 3 + 3 subs; Valencia
4; Larrosa 1 + 1 sub; Alonso 3 subs; Villa 2 subs.

Leading Scorers

1930	8 STABILE (Argentina)
	5 CEA (Uruguay)
1934	4 SCHIAVIO (Italy), CONEN (Germany) and NEJEDLY (Czechoslovakia)
1938	8 LEONIDAS (Brazil)
	7 SZENGELLER (Hungary)
	5 PIOLA (Italy)

1950   7   ADEMIR (Brazil)
       5   SCHIAFFINO (Uruguay), BASORA (Spain)

1954   11   KOCSIS (Hungary)
       6   MORLOCK (West Germany), PROBST (Austria)
       5   HUGI (Switzerland)

1958   13   FONTAINE (France)
       6   PELE (Brazil), RAHN (West Germany)
       5   VAVA (Brazil), McPARLAND (Northern Ireland)

1962   5   JERKOVIC (Yugoslavia)
       4   ALBERT (Hungary), GARRINCHA (Brazil), IVANOV (USSR), SANCHEZ (Chile), VAVA (Brazil)

1966   9   EUSEBIO (Portugal)
       5   HALLER (West Germany)
       4   HURST (England), BENE (Hungary), PORKUIAN (USSR), BECKENBAUER (West Germany)

1970   10   MULLER (West Germany)
       7   JAIRZINHO (Brazil) who scored in each game played by the Winners
       5   CUBILLAS (Peru)

1974   7   LATO (Poland)
       5   SZARMACH (Poland), NEESKENS (Holland)
       4   MULLER (West Germany), REP (Holland), EDSTROEM (Sweden)

1978   6   KEMPES (Argentina)
       5   RENSENBRINK (Holland), CUBILLAS (Peru)
       4   LUQUE (Argentina), KRANKL (Austria)

Expulsions During Previous Tournaments

URUGUAY 1930	Cierro (Argentina)
FRANCE 1938	Machados and Zeze (Brazil) Riha (Czechoslovakia)
SWITZERLAND 1954	Nilton Santos and Tozzi (Brazil) Bozsik (Hungary)
SWEDEN 1958	Bubernik (Czechoslovakia) Sipos (Hungary) Juskowiak (West Germany)
CHILE 1962	David and Ferrini (Italy)
ENGLAND 1966	Rattin (Argentina) Silva and Troche (Uruguay)
WEST GERMANY 1974	Caszely (Chile) Richards (Australia) Ndaye (Zaire) Montero Castillo (Uruguay) Luis Pereira (Brazil)
ARGENTINA 1978	Nyilasi and Toroscik (Hungary) Naninga (Holland)

Placed together the best individual goal-scoring performances in the World Cup Final tournaments go like this:

13 Fontaine 1958	7 Szengeller 1938
11 Kocsis 1954	Ademir 1950
10 Muller 1970	Jairzinho 1970
9 Eusebio 1966	Lato 1974
8 Stabile 1938	6 Probst 1954
Leonidas 1938	Morlock 1954
	Pelé 1958
	Rahn 1958

Some Records

ANTONIO CARBAJAL (Mexico) is the player to have appeared in most World Cup tournaments. He kept goal in 1950, 1954, 1958, 1962 and 1966

UWE SEELER (West Germany) is the player to have appeared in most matches playing on 21 occasions in the finals of 1958, 1962, 1966 and 1970.

MARIO ZAGALO (Brazil) is the only man so far to have played in (1958 and 1962) and managed (1970) winning teams

GEOFF HURST (England) is the only man to have scored a hat-trick in a World Cup Final but the record for scoring goals in any World Cup match is four, a feat which has been achieved on eight occasions:

GUSTAV WETTERSTROEM	Sweden v Cuba 1938
LEONIDAS DA SILVA	Brazil v Poland 1938
ERNEST WILLIMOWSKI	Poland v Brazil 1938
ADEMIR	Brazil v Sweden 1950
JUAN SCHIAFFINO	Uruguay v Bolivia 1950
SANDOR KOCSIS	Hungary v West Germany 1954
JUST FONTAINE	France v West Germany 1958
EUSEBIO	Portugal v North Korea 1966

Attendances and Goals World Cup 1930–1978

YEAR	VENUE	ATTENDANCES	AVERAGE	MATCHES	GOALS	AVERAGE
1930	URUGUAY	434,500	24,139	18	70	3.88
1934	ITALY	395,000	23,235	17	70	4.11
1938	FRANCE	483,000	26,833	18	84	4.66
1950	BRAZIL	1,337,000	60,772	22	88	4.00
1954	SWITZERLAND	943,000	36,270	26	140	5.38
1958	SWEDEN	868,000	24,800	35	126	3.60
1962	CHILE	776,000	24,250	32	89	2.78
1966	ENGLAND	1,614,677	50,458	32	89	2.78
1970	MEXICO	1,673,975	52,312	32	95	2.96
1974	WEST GERMANY	1,774,022	46,685	38	97	2.55
1978	ARGENTINA	1,610,215	42,374	38	102	2.68

Goal milestones in the World Cup

1st goal: LAURENT (France) 13 July 1930 against Mexico (4-1)
100th goal: JONASSON (Sweden) 1934 against Argentina (3-2)
200th goal: WETTERSTROEM (Sweden) 1938 against Cuba (8-0)
300th goal: CHICO (Brazil) 1950 against Spain (6-1)
400th goal: LEFTER (Turkey) 1954 against West Germany (2-7)
500th goal: RAHN (West Germany) 1958 against Czechoslovakia
(2-2)
600th goal: JERKOVIC (Yugoslavia) 1962 against Hungary (3-1)
700th goal: BOBBY CHARLTON (England) 1966 against Mexico (2-0)
800th goal: JAIRZINHO (Brazil) 1970 against England (1-0)
900th goal: YAZALDE (Argentina) 1974 against Haiti (4-1)
1000th goal: RENSENBRINK (Holland) 1978 against Scotland (2-3)
1100th goal: ....should be scored in Spain 1982

The Trophy

The Jules Rimet Trophy – won outright by the Brazilians in
1970 on account of their third victory – was designed by the
French sculptor, Abel Lafleur, stood a foot high and weighed
in the region of nine pounds of gold. The present trophy –
competed for in 1974 for the first time and known as the FIFA
World Cup – was designed by an Italian, Silvio Gazzaniga,
cost £8,000, was made in eighteen-carat gold and weighs about
ten pounds.

Only six countries have won the World Cup:

Brazil (1958, 1962 and 1970),
Italy (1934 and 1938),
Uruguay (1930 and 1950),
West Germany (1954 and 1974)
England (1966)
and Argentina (1978)

5 SUMMARY OF MATCHES IN WORLD CUP FINALS 1930–1978

	P	W	D	L	F	A
1. BRAZIL	52	33	10	9	119	56
2. *WEST GERMANY	47	28	9	10	110	68
3. ITALY	36	20	6	10	62	40
4. URUGUAY	29	14	5	10	57	39
5. ARGENTINA	29	14	5	10	55	43
6. HUNGARY	26	13	2	11	73	42
7. SWEDEN	28	11	6	11	48	46
8. ENGLAND	24	10	6	8	34	28
9. YUGOSLAVIA	25	10	5	10	45	34
10. USSR	19	10	3	6	30	21
11. HOLLAND	16	8	3	5	32	19
12. POLAND	14	9	1	4	27	17
13. AUSTRIA	18	9	1	8	33	36
14. CZECHOSLOVAKIA	22	8	3	11	32	36
15. FRANCE	20	8	1	11	43	38
16. CHILE	18	7	3	8	23	24
17. SPAIN	18	7	3	8	22	25
18. SWITZERLAND	18	5	2	11	28	44
19. PORTUGAL	6	5	0	1	17	8
20. MEXICO	24	3	4	17	21	62
21. PERU	12	4	1	7	17	25
22. SCOTLAND	11	2	4	5	12	21
23. EAST GERMANY (GDR)	6	2	2	2	5	5
24. PARAGUAY	7	2	2	3	12	19
25. UNITED STATES	7	3	0	4	12	21
26. WALES	5	1	3	1	4	4
27. NORTHERN IRELAND	5	2	1	2	6	10
28. RUMANIA	8	2	1	5	12	17
29. BULGARIA	12	0	4	8	9	29
30. TUNISIA	3	1	1	1	3	2

*(including GERMANY 1934–38)

		P	W	D	L	F	A
31.	NORTH KOREA	4	1	1	2	5	9
32.	CUBA	3	1	1	1	5	12
33.	BELGIUM	9	1	1	7	12	25
34.	TURKEY	3	1	0	2	10	11
35.	ISRAEL	3	0	2	1	1	3
36.	MOROCCO	3	0	1	2	2	6
37.	AUSTRALIA	3	0	1	2	0	5
38.	IRAN	3	0	1	2	2	8
39.	COLOMBIA	3	0	1	2	5	11
40.	NORWAY	1	0	0	1	1	2
41.	EGYPT	1	0	0	1	2	4
42.	DUTCH EAST INDIES	1	0	0	1	0	6
43.	EL SALVADOR	3	0	0	3	0	9
44.	SOUTH KOREA	2	0	0	2	0	16
45.	HAITI	3	0	0	3	2	14
46.	ZAIRE	3	0	0	3	0	14
47.	BOLIVIA	3	0	0	3	0	16

BRAZIL remain the only country to have taken part in the final stages of each of the World Cup competitions.

6 THE TEAMS WHO HAVE QUALIFIED

Important dates:

16 January – Draw for the First Round.

22 April – Lists of 40 possible players submitted by each team to FIFA.

5 June – Lists reduced to 22 players who may be used during the tournament.

The 'seeds' were given an undoubted advantage at the Draw by being selected to play all their first three matches in the same venue. ITALY in Vigo; WEST GERMANY in Gijon; ARGENTINA in Alicante (with the opening match being at Nou Camp in Barcelona); ENGLAND in Bilbao; SPAIN in Valencia; and BRAZIL in Seville.

Psychology plays an important part in football, and several teams have met previously in World Cup tournaments. POLAND beat ITALY 2–1 in 1974 and PERU 1–0 in 1978; WEST GERMANY beat CHILE 1–0 in 1974 but lost to AUSTRIA 2–3 in 1978 (although they have the satisfaction of having beaten their neighbours twice in this qualifying competition); ARGENTINA beat HUNGARY 2–1 four years ago and BELGIUM defeated EL SALVADOR 3–0 when the teams last competed in 1970; the countries in Group V have never previously met in a World Cup finals but in 1974 YUGOSLAVIA beat Spain in the qualifying competition and four years later the roles were reversed; and in Group VI BRAZIL and SCOTLAND played a goalless match in 1974 – a match which would turn out to have been between the only sides to have remained unbeaten in 1974 (SCOTLAND) and in 1978 (BRAZIL).

On the following pages is a dossier on all those teams taking part in the competition and who will hope to 'peak' during the months of June and July.

Group 1: Italy

*Federazione Italiana Giuoco Calcio founded 1898. Joined FIFA
1905. Previous appearances*: 1934 (Winners), 1938 (Winners),
1950, 1954, 1962, 1966, 1970 (Second), 1974 and 1978 (Fourth).

Present tournament: Second in European Group V behind
YUGOSLAVIA with 12 points from 8 games. Played
YUGOSLAVIA (won 2–0 at home and drew 1–1 away),
DENMARK (won 2–0 at home and lost 1–3 away), GREECE
(won 2–0 away and drew 1–1 at home) and LUXEMBOURG
(won 2–0 away and 1–0 at home.

The manager and players: ENZO BEARZOT (54) became sole
manager of Italy in October 1977, steered his side to Fourth place
in the previous World Cup. After gaining four 2–0 victories in the late
months of 1980, the team lost in June against Denmark, scraped two
1–1 draws and only beat Luxembourg 1–0 in December thanks to a
goal by a defender after qualification had already been assured.
DINO ZOFF (40) is still in goal and the defence has been stable for
the last three years with CLAUDIO GENTILE (28), FULVIO
COLLOVATI (25 on 9 May) as stopper, GAETANO SCIREA (29
on 25 May) as *libero* and ANTONIO CABRINI (24) as left-back.
PIETRO VIERCHOWOD (23 on 6 April) and GIUSEPPE
BARESI (24) have also played recently. MARCO TARDELLI (27)
is still playing aggressively in midfield, GIANCARLO
ANTOGNONI (28 on 1 April) received a head-injury last
November but hopes to be recovered in time and GIUSEPPE
DOSSENA (24 on 2 May) has recently played as a schemer.
BRUNO CONTI (27) is a speedy wing, ROBERTO BETTEGA
(30) is a forward of great technique and fearsome heading power, but
how badly Italy want back PAOLO ROSSI (25) after serving two
years banishment for being involved in a match-fixing scheme (more
as dupe than real participant). ROBERTO PRUZZO (27 on 1 April)
scores goals freely in league games but FRANCESCO GRAZIANI
(29) has been more favoured of late and his colleague at Fiorentina,
ERALDO PECCI (27 on 12 April) might squeeze in as an
imaginative playmaker. The leading goalscorer was GRAZIANI
with 3.

Poland

Polski Zwiazek Pilki Niznej (PZPN) founded in 1919. Joined FIFA 1923

Previous appearances: 1938, 1974 (Third) and 1978 (Second Round).

Present tournament: Headed European Group VII over EAST GERMANY (won 1–0 at home and 3–2 away) and MALTA (won 2–0 away – game suspended for crowd trouble – and 6–0 at home. 8 points from 4 games.

The manager and players: ANTONI PIECHNIZEK (41), was appointed manager in January 1981 and has speedily blended in some promising new talent with older, more experienced players. In these four games he used three goalkeepers PIETR MOWLIK (30), JOSEF MYLNARCZYK (28) as well as JAN TOMASEWSKI (34) who has been playing for Hercules Alicante and whose advice will be of great use. WLADYSLAW ZMUDA (28 on 5 June) is one of the most experienced of central defenders in Europe, MAREK DZIUBA (26) is a very effective rightback who has played in midfield, JAN JALOCHA (26 on 4 April) has come in at leftback and PAWEL JANAS (29) has been in the centre, but TADEUSZ DOLNY (20) is a newcomer who has been most impressive playing there. ZBIGNIEW BONIEK (26) had a splendid tournament in 1978 as a creative midfield player, WALDEMAR MATYSIK (21) has recently been blooded as have STANISLAV SKROBOWSKI (21). STEFAN MAJEWSKI (26) and ANDREZ BUNCOL (22). GREGORZ LATO (32 on 8 April) has fallen back from the attack to make deep runs from midfield, ANDREZ SZARMACH (31) is still foraging up front but there are new names in ANDREZ IWAN (22), WLODEK SMOLAREK (25 on 16 July), ANDREZ PALASZ (21), MIROSLAV OKONSKI (23) and DARIUSZ DZIE-KANOWSKI (19). SMOLAREK scored 5 of the 12 goals in the qualifying tournament.

Peru

Federacion Peruana de Futbo1. Founded 1922. Joined FIFA 1922.

Previous appearances: 1930, 1970 (Quarter-finalists) and 1978 (Second Round).

Present tournament: Headed South American Group II with 6 points from 4 games: ahead of URUGUAY (won 2–1 away and drew 0–0 at home) and COLOMBIA (Drew 1–1 away and won 2–0 at home).

The manager and players: The coach of the successful 1970 side was DIDI and on this occasion it is another Brazilian who has steered Peru through. 'TIM' (born as ELBA DE PADUA LIMA, 71 years ago) took over in 1981 before the qualifying tournament and, appalled at the level of local club football, immediately summoned back many players who had taken their skills overseas. RAMON QUIROGA (31) is still playing in goal, often living up to his nickname of 'El Loco', and several other members of the defence on show in Argentina are still playing. That inextinguishable stopper HECTOR CHUMPITAZ (who claims to be only 38 on 12 April) is still at the heart of the defence alongside TORIBIO DIAZ (29) with JAIME DUARTE (28) at right-back and ROBERTO ROJAS (26) at left. JORGE OLAECHEA (23) is a youngster who has been on very good form recently, as is EDUARDO MALASQUEZ (24), but the most impressive newcomer to the side is JULIO CESAR URIBE (24) who is a decisive runner in midfield. Alongside him are CESAR CUETO (28), who was called back from Nacional of Colombia for the qualifying games, as was JOSE VELASQUEZ (29) from Toronto Blizzard. The happily-named GERONIMO BARBADILLO (29) dribbles skilfully down one wing, JUAN OBLITAS (30), who has been playing in Belgium is still in fine form – both providing a service for GUILLERMO LA ROSA (27) who scored two of the five goals as did URIBE. And there is still that favourite from 1970 and 1978 TEOFILO CUBILLAS (who was 33 on 8 March and who has played in Europe) to cause alarm with his elegant running and fierce shooting, which brought him 5 goals in each of those competitions. Peru have been in training for six months and are bound to cause more than one surprise – for the third time running!

Cameroon

Federation Camerounaise de Football founded 1960. Joined FIFA 1962.

Cameroon, a large country on the west coast of Africa sandwiched between Zaire to the south and Nigeria to the north, is making its first appearance in a finals. In African knockout section beat MALAWI (won 3–0 at home and drew 1–1 away), ZIMBABWE (won 2–0 at home and lost 0–1 away), ZAIRE (won 1–0 away and 6–1 at home) and MOROCCO (won 2–0 away and 2–1 at home).

The manager and players : A Yugoslav, 40-year old BRANKO ZUTIC, who was appointed manager in August 1980, has drawn on the talents of the leading club side in the country, Canon Yaundé. THOMAS N'KONO (26) whose heroes are Lev Yachin, Gordon Banks and Peter Shilton may be the best goalkeeper to come out of Africa in recent years, and as his deputy he has ANTOINE BELL (27), who has taken his talents to play in France. French-based are also the right-back MICHEL KAHAM (31 on 1 June) and the stopper IBRAHIM AOUDOU (25), but locally-based defenders are FRANCOIS N'DOUMBE LEA (27), EFFEM M'BOM (26), GILBERT AKONO (27) and JACQUES KINGUE (25) although the latter has recently been injured. The midfield is full of home-based players. THEOPHILE ABEGA (26) is the playmaker of the team and has with him the experienced JEAN PIERRE TOKOTO (33) and GREGOIRE M'BIDA (23), but it is in the forward line where we come across the real star of the team, ROGER MILLA (30 on 20 May) who moved to play in France in 1977, had an unhappy time but is scoring regularly for the Corsican side of Bastia, which he joined two seasons ago. JACQUES N'GUEA (26) is a lively forward, JEAN MANGA ONGUENE (35) is the grand old man of football in Cameroon, and PAUL BAHOKEN (27 on 7 July) is an incisive winger. MILLA scored 6 goals during the qualifying competition, and voted African Footballer of the Year were MILLA for 1976, N'KONO for 1979 and MANGA ONGUENE for 1980.

Group 2: West Germany

Deutscher Fussball-Bund founded in 1900. Joined FIFA 1904–1945, 1950.

Previous appearances (including pre-war Germany): 1934 (Third), 1938, 1954 (Winners), 1958 (Fourth), 1962 (Quarter-finalists), 1966 (Second), 1970 (Third), 1974 (Winners) and 1978 (Second round).

Present tournament: Headed European Group I with 16 points from 8 games over AUSTRIA (won 2–0 at home and 3–1 away), BULGARIA (won 3–1 away and 4–0 at home), ALBANIA (won 2–0 away and 8–0 at home) and FINLAND (won 4–0 away and 7–1 at home). A staggering 33 goals for and only 3 against!

The manager and players: JUPP DERWALL, who was 55 on 10 March, took over as manager in July 1978 and steered the team to victory in the 1980 European Nations Championship. HARALD SCHUMACHER (28) is the undisputed first choice as goalkeeper. MANNY KALTZ (29) is a marvellous counter-attacking right-back, KARL HEINZ FORSTER (23) an authoritative stopper, ULRICH STIELKE (27) who plays for Real Madrid is a skilful sweeper and HANS PETER BRIEGEL (26) an awesome defender wherever he plays. RAINER BONHOF (30) has valuable experience of playing for Valencia, PAUL BREITNER (30) is performing masterfully in midfield and also has experience of Spain, playing for Real Madrid, HANSI MÜLLER (24) is a left-sided player who should recover speedily after undergoing an operation for cartilage trouble. BERND SCHUSTER (22) might still be integrated since his transfer two seasons ago to Barcelona, and KLAUS ALLOFS (25) has played deeper since the dazzling debut of PIERRE LITTBARSKI (22 on 16 April) in the forward line. The svelte KLAUS FISCHER (32) and the large-boned HORST HRUBESCH (31 on 17 April) make a fearsome pair of central attackers, in addition to KARL-HEINZ RUMMENIGGE (26), probably the most lethal striker in Europe. Of those 33 goals he scored 9, FISCHER 7, KALTZ 5 and LITTBARSKI 3.

Algeria

Federation Algerienne de Football founded 1962. Joined FIFA 1963.

Previous appearances: None.

Present tournament: Beat SIERRA LEONE (drew 2–2 away, won 3–1 at home), SUDAN (won 2–0 at home, drew 1–1 away), NIGER (won 4–0 at home, lost 0–1 away) and NIGERIA (won 2–0 away and 2–1 at home).

The manager and players: The 52-year old Russian, YEVGENI ROGOV, took over as manager in July 1981 after much advice had been given by French and Yugoslav coaches. Although several key players are abroad with clubs in either France or Belgium, this experience should be of considerable value. Not surprisingly, Rogov has chosen to build a firm defensive base and to counter-attack quickly through a packed midfield. Goalkeepers he has chosen have been MEHDI CERBAH (29) and, in reserve, YACIN BENTAMAA but the defence is experienced with SALAH LARBES (30) as right-back, FAUZI MANSOURI (26) at left-back, and in the centre are two players of high talent, MAHEOUD MAHMOUD (29) and the tall stopper NOEDINE KOURICHI (28 on 12 April) who plays for Bordeaux. Reserves are ABDEL KADER HORR (29), ABDEL DJADOUI (26) and MUSTAPHA KOUICI (27). The star of the team is LAKHDAR BELLOUMI (24) a most inspired midfield player who was voted African Footballer of the Year for 1981. Other midfield players are RABAH MADJER (24), MOHAMMED KACI-SAID (24) and the experienced BOUZID MAHIOUZ (29), FETHI CHEBEL (26), RABAH GAMOUH (30) and MUSTAFA DAHLEB (30), the last three based in France. In attack there is DANIEL ZIDANE (27 on 28 April) who plays in Belgium, SALAH ASSAD (24) and SAID HAMINI (22 on 7 May), who is a young winger of considerable potential. Algeria should acquit itself well in these finals.

Austria

Oesterreichischer Fussball-Bund founded in 1904. Joined FIFA 1905.

Previous appearances: 1934 (Fourth), 1954 (Third), 1958 and 1978 (Second Round).

Present tournament: Second in European Group I with 11 points from 8 games behind WEST GERMANY (lost 0–2 away and 1–3 at home), but before BULGARIA (won 2–0 at home, drew 0–0 away), ALBANIA (won 1–0 away and 5–0 at home) and FINLAND (won 2–0 away and 5–1 at home).

The manager and players: KARL STOTZ, 55, saw Austria through the qualifying rounds only to be dismissed in December 1981 and succeeded by GEORGE SCHMIDT. There are two experienced goalkeepers in FRIEDRICH KONCILIA (34) and HERBERT FEURER (27), and at the centre of the defence is the tall, powerful BRUNO PEZZEY (27) with alongside him HERBERT WEBER (26). The full-backs have been BERND KRAUSS (24) on the right and DIETER MIRNEGG (28 on 24 May) on the left, but JOHAN DIHANIC (23) has played recently and could come into contention for a place. It is when we move forward that we realise how many Austrian players are serving abroad. HERBERT PROHASKA (26) is with Internazionale of Milan, KURT JARA (31) has been to both West Germany and Switzerland, REINHOLD HINTERMAIER (26) plays in West Germany but ERICH HATTENBERGER (33), ERNST BAUMIESTER (24) and HELMUT WARTINGER (22) are still based in Austria. HANS KRANKL (29) has recently returned after spending some time playing in Spain for Barcelona, WALTER SCHACHNER (25) is playing in Italy, KURT WELZL (27) is scoring goals for Valencia but three new talents have appeared on the scene MAX HAGMAYR (27), GERNOT JURTIN (26) and HERMANN STADLER (21) who is a fast and tricky runner. CHRISTIAN KEGLEVITS (20) is another forward of great promise.

Chile

Federacion de Football de Chile founded in 1895. Joined FIFA in 1912.

Previous appearances: 1934, 1950, 1962 (Third), 1966 and 1974.

Present tournament: Headed South American Group III with 7 points from 4 games over ECUADOR (drew 0–0 away and won 2–0 at home) and PARAGUAY (won 1–0 away and 3–0 at home).

The manager and players: LUIS SANTIBANEZ, 45, took over as manager in 1977 (his first game being the defeat by SCOTLAND on 15 June of that year) and has worked hard to blend together experience and youthful promise. MARIO OSBEN (32 on 14 July) let in no goals during the four matches of the qualifying competition and has as a reserve OSCAR WIRTH (26). Another experienced player, ELIAS FIGUEROA (35), organizes the defence and has alongside him EDUARDO VALENZUELA (24), with LIZARDO GARRIDO (24) and MANUEL BIGORRA (25) as full-backs, cover coming from MARIO SOTO (30), ENZO ESCOBAR (30) and OSVALDO VARGAS (24). The midfield has been the weakest of the departments due to an injury to MANUEL ROJAS (28) but EDUARDO BONVALLET (26), RUDOLFO DUBO, CARLOS RIVAS (28), and MIGUEL NEIRA (29) have played there. It is among the forwards, however, that most promise has been shown. PATRIZIO YANEZ (21) is a goalscoring winger, RODRIGO SANTANDER (22) and JOSE LUIS ALVAREZ (21) have shown themselves to be players of skill, but the main threat comes from CARLOS CAZELLY (32 on 5 July) who played in the 1974 tournament and subsequently took his talents to Spain, scoring goals for Levante of Valencia and Espanol of Barcelona. Overall experience of European conditions this side may lack but as with every South American country the players will have been together for several months. The goalscorers were YANEZ and CAZELLY 2, NEIRA and RIVAS 1.

Group 3: Argentina

Asociacion de Futbol Argentino founded in 1893. Joined FIFA in 1912.

Previous appearances: 1930 (Runners-up), 1934, 1958, 1962, 1966 (Quarter-finalists), 1974 (Second Round) and 1978 (Winners).

Present tournament: Qualify automatically as reigning champions.

The manager and players: CESAR LUIS MENOTTI, 51 in November next, took over as manager soon after the 1974 World Cup and led his team to victory in the following tournament held in Argentina. He has kept faith with many members of that side. UBALDO FILLOL (32 on 21 July) is still the first-choice goalkeeper and the defence is the same with JORGE OLGUIN (30 on 17 May) at right-back, LUIS GALVAN (33) at stopper, DANIEL PASSARELLA (29 on 25 May) as a sweeper who likes to attack and ALBERTO TARANTINI (26) returned home from a season spent in England with Birmingham City at left-back. JOSE VAN TUYNE (27) and JULIO OLARTICOECHEA (23) are others who have recently played. Turning to midfield OSWALDO ARDILES (28) who also brought his talents to England, but this time to stay, will have alongside him MARIO KEMPES (28 on 15 July) who has returned to Argentina after having spent four seasons with Valencia and AMERICO GALLEGO (27 on 25 April). The real difference in the side is in front. DIEGO MARADONA (21) is a truly remarkable footballer of prodigious talents, and RAMON DIAZ (22) can play as an out :and-out striker or in an attacking role from midfield. DANIEL BERTONI (27) has been scoring goals for Fiorentina in Italy and prior to this was with Seville in Spain. Two further young players who have recently made their mark have been LUIS AMUCHASTEGUI (23) in the attack and PATRICIO HERNANDEZ (25) in midfield. Argentina have known some poor form in recent months but with a KEMPES returned to his best and with a MARADONA who is capable of anything they are capable of performing extremely well.

Belgium

Union Royale Belge des Societes de Football Association founded 1895. Joined FIFA 1904.

Previous appearances: 1930, 1934, 1938, 1954 and 1970.

Present tournament: Headed European Group II above FRANCE (lost 2–3 away and won 2–0 at home), EIRE (drew 1–1 away and won 1–0 at home), HOLLAND (won 1–0 at home and lost 0–3 away) and CYPRUS (won 2–0 away and 3–2 at home).

The manager and players: Shrewd GUY THYS, who was 59 last August, was appointed in August 1977 and steered Belgium to the final of the 1980 European Nations Championship. That particular competition gave a golden opportunity for building up a team for this World Cup. JEAN-MARIE PFAFF (28) and MICHEL PREUD'HOMME (23) are two respected goal-keepers, and the defence has played together for the past two seasons: ERIC GERETS (28 on 18 May) an outstanding right-back, MICHEL RENQUIN (26) is a cultured left-back and LOU MILLECAMPS (30) has played as central defender with WALTER MEEUWS (31 on 11 July). MARC BAECKE (26 on 24 July) is a most promising full-back. There has been some instability in midfield owing to the ageing of WILFRID VAN MOER (37 on 1 March) and injuries to LUDO COECK (26) but RAYMOND MOMMENS (23) has done well, FRANK VERCAUTEREN (25) and ALBERT CLUYTENS (26) have played and RENE VANDEREYCKEN (29 on 22 July) is powerful with a fierce left-foot shot and JUAN LOZANO (26) has recently become naturalized. FRANCOIS VAN DER ELST (27) has returned from the States, JAN CEULEMANS (25) and ERWIN VANDENBERGH (23) are both scoring fre-quently and last September two further young forwards appeared who play with skill and aggression: ALEX CZERNIATYSKY (21 on 28 July) and EDDY VOORDECKERS (22). There can be no doubt that Belgium are one of the most efficient sides in Europe. Leading scorers were ERWIN VANDENBERGH with 5 goals and JAN CEULEMANS with 4.

Hungary

Magyar Labdarugok Szovetsege. Founded 1901. Joined FIFA 1907.

Previous appearances: 1934, 1938 (beaten finalists), 1954 (beaten finalists), 1958, 1962 (Quarter-finalists), 1966 (Quarter-finalists) and 1978.

Present tournament: Headed European Group IV with 10 points from 8 games, ahead of ENGLAND (lost 1–3 at home and 0–1 away), RUMANIA (won 1–0 at home and drew 0–0 away), SWITZERLAND (drew 2–2 away and won 3–0 at home) and NORWAY (won 2–1 away and 4–1 at home).

The manager and players: 41-year old KALMAN MESZOLY, appointed manager in May 1980, played 61 times for his country between 1961 and 1971 at centre-back and took part in the World Cup Finals of 1962 and 1966, with Florian Albert among his team-mates. He began 1981 by watching Hungary beat Spain 3–0 in Valencia before playing the eight games of the qualifying tournament in just over six months. FERENC MEZAROS (32 on 11 April) displaced BELA KATZIRZ (27) in goal, played in the 1978 finals and now works for Malcolm Allison with Sporting Lisbon. The defence mixes experience and youthful enthusiasm, with GYOZO MARTOS (32) at right-back, JOSZEF TOTH (31) and LASZLO BALINT (34) – who plays in France – at the centre, alongside IMRE GARABA (24), with ATTILA KEREKES (28) and GABOR SZANTO (23) also on call. In midfield is SANDOR SALLAI (22), who can both mark tightly as well as cleverly suggest openings, KAROLY CSAPO (30), TIBOR RAB (26) and SANDOR MULLER (33) who has been playing for Hercules Alicante in Spain and others who will come into consideration. But the real star of midfield is the tall TIBOR NYILASI (27) who regularly scores goals and links well with that other outstanding Hungarian player, the central striker ANDRAS TOROCSIK (27 on 1 May), whose ball-control and passing are exceptional. Alongside him are LASZLO FAZEKAS (35) who first played in 1968 and who is often substituted late in a game by BELA BODONYI (26), and the chief scorer was LASZLO KISS (26) with 4 of the 13 goals in the qualifying competition, other leading scorers being FAZEKAS with 3 and NYILASI and BALINT both with two.

El Salvador

Federacion Salvadorena de Futbo. Founded 1935. Joined FIFA 1938.

Previous appearance: 1970.

Present tournament: Finished Second in CONCACAF Hexagonal play-off held in Honduras with 6 points from 5 games against HONDURAS (0–0), MEXICO (won 1–0), CANADA (lost 0–1), CUBA (drew 0–0) and HAITI (won 1–0).

The manager and players: It's almost a miracle that any serious sport has survived in this war-shattered country where in the past two and a half years almost 40,000 people have lost their lives. There was trouble sparked off by football when El Salvador last qualified for these finals – war broke out for ten days between this country and Honduras following victory in the qualifying competition, the scorer of the crucial goal being the present manager of the side, 36-year old MAURICIO RODRIGUEZ, who took his players to the United States for several months at the start of 1981. He has an outstanding goalkeeper in RICARDO GUEVARA MORA (20) who might be forced to play a bit in Spain, and the defence will be drawn from JOSE FRANCISCO JOVEL (25), JAIME ALBERTO RODRIGUEZ (23), EDUARDO OSORIO (25) a most determined tackler, MIGUEL ANGEL AREVALO (25) and the experienced CARLOS HUMBERTO RECINOS (29). The star of the team is JOSE NORBERT HUEZO (26) the captain and inspirator of play from the right of midfield and his allies in suggesting play will be MAURICIO ALBERTO ALFARO (28), JOSE LUIS RUGAMAS (27) and ALONSO VENTURA (24). In the attack will be MAURICIO QUINTANILLA (26), MIGUEL GONZALES (25) and his younger brother JORGE ALBERTO GONZALES (21), known locally as 'El Magico', and compared to Diego Maradona and Johann Cruyff! That only two goals were scored by El Salvador in these five games (and one of those from a dubious penalty) suggests that the attack is weak; however the fact that only one goal was allowed through also suggests that the defence is resolute.

Group 4: England

Football Association founded 1863. Joined FIFA 1905–1920, 1924–1928, 1946.

Previous appearances: 1950, 1954 (Quarter-finalists), 1958, 1962 (Quarter-finalists), 1966 (Winners) and 1970 (Quarter-finalists).

Present tournament: Second in European Group IV with 9 points from 8 games against HUNGARY (won 3–1 away and 1–0 at home), RUMANIA (lost 1–2 away and drew 0–0 at home), SWITZERLAND (won 2–1 at home and lost 1–2 away) and NORWAY (won 4–0 and lost 1–2 away).

The manager and players: RON GREENWOOD, 60, took over as manager in August 1977. Hopes seeming to have been blighted on three occasions, but England's good fortune held and the team squeezed through to Spain. PETER SHILTON (32) and RAY CLEMENCE (33) have served as fine goalkeepers, PHIL NEAL (31) and MICK MILLS (33) as full-backs, but maybe KENNY SANSOM (23) will win back his place at left-back. PHIL THOMPSON (28), ALVIN MARTIN (24) and DAVE WATSON (35) have been centre backs. TREVOR BROOKING (33) is a left-sided midfield player of enormous cunning, BRYAN ROBSON (25) is a defensive midfielder of class and RAY WILKINS (25), although out through injury recently, is returning to drive forward on the right. GLENN HODDLE (24) is an attacking midfield player who can both pass immaculately and shoot fiercely when near goal and TERRY McDERMOTT (30) scored three times during the qualifying rounds, as did centre-forward PAUL MARINER. TREVOR FRANCIS (28 on 19 April) appears to have recovered all his sharpness prior to an Achilles tendon injury. KEVIN KEEGAN (31) has found new zest to add to his undoubted footballing ability. TONY MORLEY made a spectacular debut in the return match against Hungary at Wembley in November 1981, and on the other wing there is STEVE COPPELL (27 on 9 July) who has the benefit of playing alongside both Robson and Wilkins for Manchester United.

France

Federation Francaise de Football. Founded 1919. Joined FIFA 1904.

Previous appearances: 1930, 1934, 1938, 1954, 1958 (Third), 1966 and 1978.

Present tournament: Second in European Group II with 10 points from 8 games ahead of EIRE on goal difference (20/8 over 17/11). Behind BELGIUM (lost 2–3 away and won 2–0 at home), EIRE (won 2–0 at home and lost 2–3 away), HOLLAND (lost 0–1 away and won 2–0 at home) and CYPRUS (won 7–0 away and 4–0 at home).

The manager and the players: MICHEL HIDALGO, 49 on 22 March, took over as manager at the start of 1976 and steered the team to the last finals. He has two relatively inexperienced but promising goalkeepers in JEAN CASTANEDA (25) and PATRICK HIZARD (27) but elsewhere there is a familiar look about the defence, with GERARD JANVION (28) and MAXIME BOSSIS (27 on 26 June) as full-backs, with PATRICK BATTISTON (25) in reserve. CHRISTIAN LOPEZ (29) and that elegant sweeper MARIUS TRESOR (32) are still formidable in the centre of the defence, with LEONARD SPECHT (28) and JEAN-LUC RUTY (23 on 5 July) in reserve MICHEL PLATINI (27 on 21 June) is the most exciting player France has produced for twenty years, and in midfield alongside him will be his club colleague JEAN-FRANCOIS LARIOS (25), JEAN AMADOU TIGANA (27 on 23 June), ALAIN GIRESSE (29) or BERNHARD GENGHINI (24). In the attack DOMINIQUE ROCHETEAU (27) has forsaken the right flank to play more as a central attacker, but JACQUES ZIMAKO (29) has counter-attacked most efficiently down the right, whilst on the left there is still DIDIER SIX (27), a truly dazzling player, with as his deputy the exciting BRUNO BELLONE (20). In the centre there is still BERNARD LACOMBE (29). But injuries have cast a blight on the progress of the French team and Hidalgo will be praying for better fortune in Spain. PLATINI scored 4 times, SIX and LACOMBE 3 each.

Czechoslovakia

Ceskoslovensky Fotbalovy Svaz founded in 1901. Joined FIFA 1906.

Previous appearances: 1934 (Second), 1938 (Quarter-finalists), 1954, 1958, 1962 (Second) and 1970.

Present tournament: Second in European Group III with 10 points from 8 games ahead of WALES on goal difference. Played RUSSIA (lost 0–1 away and drew 1–1 at home), WALES (lost 0–1 away and won 2–0 at home), ICELAND (won 6–1 at home and drew 1–1 away) and TURKEY (won 2–0 at home and 3–0 away).

The manager and players: JOSEF VENGLOS (54) took over as manager in August 1968 and steered the team to third place in the 1980 European Nations Championship after the team had beaten the hosts, Italy, on penalties. STANISLAV SEMAN (29) and ZDENEK HRUSKA (28 on 25 July) have played as goalkeepers but the defence has an experienced look about it with PREMYL BICOVSKY (31), ROTISLAV VOJACEK (33), LADISLAV JURKEMIK (29 on 20 July), JOZEF BARMOS (27) and LIBOR RADIMEC (31) all having played well into the past with JAN FIALA (26 on 19 May) and FRANTISEK JAKUBEC (26), an overlapping full-back, the real newcomers. In midfield there is also an emphasis on experience. ANTONIN   PANENKA   (33)   and   FRANTISEK STAMBACHER (29) have now been joined by MARIAN MASNY (31) who has taken his skills deeper further back. JAN BERGER (26), LADISLAV VIZEK (27), JAN KOZAK (28 on 17 April) and LUDEK MACELA (31) are others who have been selected recently. PETR JANECKA (26), TOMAS KRIZ (22) and WERNER LICKA (27), a left-winger of skill, are newcomers to the attack but the principal threat still comes from ZDENEK NEHODA (30 on 9 May) who is an opportunist of great flair. The principal goal-scorers were KOZAK 4, NEHODA 3, VIZEK and LICKA and JANECKA with 2 each.

Kuwait

Kuwait Football Association founded 1952. Joined FIFA 1962.
   Previous appearances: None.
   Present tournament: Headed Group in Asia-Oceania section
with wins over SOUTH KOREA (6–0), MALAYSIA (4–0) and
THAILAND (2–0) and final playoff ahead of NEW ZEALAND
(won 2–1 away and drew 2–2 at home), CHINA (lost 0–3 away
and won 1–0 at home) and SAUDI ARABIA (won 1–0 away and
2–0 at home).
   The manager and players: This achievement was a personal
triumph for the Brazilian coach, CARLOS ALBERTO
PARREIRA (39) who is NOT the former Brazilian full-back,
but the man who took over as coach after MARIO ZAGALO
when he left after serving for two years in 1978. His first
noteworthy deed was to steer Kuwait to the Quarter-final stage of
the 1980 Olympics, in which the team was beaten by the hosts,
Russia. The first-choice goalkeeper AHMED AL TARABULSI
(35) was a hero of that particular tournament and will be joined
by ABDULLAH MAAYUF (28) as stopper, NAYEEM
SAAD (26) as right-back, WALEED AL JASSEM (24) as left-
back, MAHBOUB JOMAH (26) as an experienced central
defender and HAMOUD ELEITAH (22), a young defender of
great promise. The captain, SAAD AL HOUTI (27), plays in
midfield receiving support from ABDULLAH BALOUSHI
(21), MOHAMMED KARAM (25) who is a skilful inside-
forward, NASSER AL GHANEM (21) and AHMED ASKAR
(21), who can also play in defence. But the most experienced
members of the side are in the forward line. YASSIM JACOUB
(28) regularly scores goals, ABDUL AZIZ AL ANBARI (28) has
been in punishing form lately, FATHI KAMAL (26) leads the
forwards with skill and FAISAL AL DEKEEL (25) is expert at
making scything runs from midfield. There are only 14 fulltime
clubs in Kuwait and less than 1,700 registered players, all of them
'amateurs', but the riches which have flowed in from exporting
oil have been spent very wisely.

Group 5: Spain

Real Federacion Espanola de Futbol, founded 1913. Joined FIFA 1904.

Previous appearances: 1934 (Quarter-finalists), 1950 (Fourth), 1962, 1966 and 1978.

Present tournament: Qualify automatically as hosts.

The manager and players: JOSE EMILIO SANTAMARIA, 53 on 31 July, took over as manager in succession to LADISLAV KUBALA in August 1980 and has played many 'friendlies' in the past two years against teams from Europe as well as going on a tour of South America in the June and July of 1981. He has a talented goalkeeper in LUIS ARCONADA (28 on 26 June) who will be supported by JAVIER GONZALEZ URRUTICOECHEA (30) and FRANCISCO BUYO (24). He has played several matches with the same defence. JOSE ANTONIO CAMACHO (27 on 8 June), MIGUEL TENDILLO (21) as stopper, JOSE RAMON ALESANCO (26) as sweeper and RAFAEL GORDILLO (26) as left-back. ANTONIO MACEDA (25), CUNDI (24), MIGUEL JIMENEZ (23) and GENARO CELAYETA (27) have made the occasional appearance. JESUS ZAMORA (27) is very much the play-maker in midfield and has been supported by MIGUEL ALONSO (29), JOAQUIN (26 on 9 June) or VICTOR (25) who is a tireless runner throughout a game. In the forwards are JUANITO (27), his colleague with Real Madrid SANTILLANA (29), DANI (31 on 28 June), JESUS SATRUSTEGUI (28) and his club-colleague with Real Sociedad ROBERTO LOPEZ UFARTE (24), who plays on the left of the field. Wing forwards who have recently given telling displays include MARCOS (22) on the left and ENRIQUE SAURA on the right. There is further space given to Spain at the end of the book.

Honduras

Federacion Nacional Deportiva Extraescolaro. Founded 1951. Joined FIFA 1951.

Present tournament : Never having qualified before, Honduras were given a tremendous boost when it was decided that the country could host the six-nation play-offs to decide which two countries from CONCACAF (Confederacion Norte Centroamericana y del Caribe de Futbol) could progress to Spain. Having trained together for two years, it was no surprise that Honduras came through gaining wins over Haiti (4–0), Cuba (2–0) and Canada (2–1) as well as two goalless draws against El Salvador and Mexico, who were unable to force a victory that would have taken them through. Yet again!

The manager and players: The manager is 39-year old 'CHELATO' HERRERA, who has concentrated his interest on three or four local club sides. JULIO ARZU (25) is first-choice goalkeeper and let in only one goal in those five games with JIMMY STEWARD (35) and OSCAR BENEGAS in reserve. The defence is well marshalled by an authoritative 'stopper' ANTON COSTLY (26), but also playing in Spain is another talented central defender in GILBERTO YEARWOOD (23). EFRAIN GUTIERREZ (22), JAIME VILLEGAS (31), HECTOR ZELAYA (23), HERMAN GARCIA (27) and DOMINGO DRUMMOND (23) are others in consideration for defensive places. DAVID BUESO (23) is an attacking midfield player on the left of the midfield, SALVADOR BERNANDEZ (26), JAVIER TOLEDO (26) and JUAN MURILLO (24) have also been selected, but the real footballer in the team is RAMON MARADIAGA (26), known locally as 'El Primitivo', who plays with all the determination of a Nobby Stiles or a Romeo Benetti, to mention only two of the folk-heroes of recent times. ROBERTO FIGUEROA (22) and JIMMY BAILEY (20) have been scoring regularly in the forward line.

Yugoslavia

Fudbalski Savez Jugoslavije founded 1919. Joined FIFA 1919.

Previous appearances: 1930 (Semi-finalists), 1950, 1954 (Quarter-finalists), 1958 (Quarter-finalists), 1962 (Fourth) and 1974 (Second Round).

Present tournament: Headed European Group V with 13 points from 8 games ahead of ITALY (lost 0–2 away and drew 1–1 at home), DENMARK (won 2–1 at home and 2–1 away), GREECE (won 5–1 at home and 2–1 away) and LUXEMBOURG (won 5–0 at home and 5–0 away).

The manager and players: Fast-talking MILJAN MILJANIC, 52 on 4 May, steered Yugoslavia to and through the 1974 World Cup finals and then left to help look after the fortunes of Real Madrid. He rejoined Yugoslavia in November 1978 and set to work to build up a squad for the World Cup. DRAGAN PANTELIC (30) is a polished goalkeeper who is a specialist at taking penalties. ZORAN VUJOVIC (23), ZLATO KRMPOTIC (23) and NENAD STOJOVIC (26) have played as full-backs, VELIMIR ZAJEC (26) as sweeper, and the stopper role has been taken by MILOS HRSTIC (26) or IVAN GUDELJ (22). Three heroes who were in the team eight years ago are still playing superbly: IVAN BULJAN (32) in defence, VLADIMIR PETROVIC (27 on 1 July) as a play-maker and IVICA SURJAK (29) as a midfielder who regularly scores goals. Two other players currently in France with Surjak are EDHEM SLIJVO (31) and the tall central attacker, VALID HALIHOZDIC (29). MILOS SESTIC (23), PREDRAG PASIC (23) a skilful winger and SAFET SUSIC (27) are others who will be in contention with ZLATO VULOVIC (twin brother to Zoran), a winger who scored 7 of the 22 Yugoslavian goals in the qualifying tournament. Yugoslavia has a decided ace in the hand – the knowledge concerning Spanish conditions assimilated by MILJANIC during his spell there.

Northern Ireland

Irish Football Association. Founded 1880. Joined FIFA 1911–1920, 1924–1928, 1946.

Previous appearance: 1958 (Quarter-finalists).

Present tournament: Second in European Group VI with 9 points from 8 games: behind SCOTLAND (drew 1–1 away and 0–0 at home), before SWEDEN (won 3–0 at home, lost 0–1 away), PORTUGAL (lost 0–1 away, won 1–0 at home) and ISRAEL (drew 0–0 away and won 1–0 at home).

The manager and players: BILLY BINGHAM, who is 51, has first-hand experience of a World Cup since in 1958 he played on the wing for Northern Ireland in Sweden. In fact he won 56 caps for his country between 1951 and 1963 and made a marvellous reappearance as manager of Northern Ireland for the second spell when his country won the Home International Championship in 1980. In PAT JENNINGS (37 on 12 June) and JIM PLATT (29) he has two excellent goalkeepers, and his defence is a neat mixture of experience and youthful enthusiasm. JIMMY NICHOLL (25) is a right-back who can make surging runs into the attack, and in the centre CHRIS NICHOLL (35) and JOHN O'NEILL (22) have built up a useful partnership. JOHN McCLELLAND (25) and MAL DONAGHY (24) compete for the left-back place with SAMMY NELSON (32). The midfield has been stable recently with MARTIN O'NEILL (30) and SAMMY McILROY (27) playing alongside DAVID McCREERY (24) or TOM CASSIDY (30). GERRY ARMSTRONG (28 on 23 May) has usually led the attack supported by NOEL BROTHERSTON (25) on the left and either TERRY COCHRANE (26) or BILLY HAMILTON (25 on 9 May) on the right. It's a small squad but has the undoubted advantage of being a compact unit playing with a special sense of pride.

Group 6: Brazil

Confederacao Brasileira do Futebol founded in 1914. Joined FIFA in 1923.

Previous appearances: 1930, 1934, 1938 (Third), 1950 (Second), 1958 (Winners), 1962 (Winners), 1966, 1970 (Winners), 1974 (Fourth) and 1978 (Third).

Present tournament: Headed South American Group I with 8 points from 4 matches: BOLIVIA (won 2–1 away and 3–1 at home) and VENEZUALA (won 1–0 away and 5–0 at home). ZICO scored 5, SOCRATES and TITA 2 each.

The manager and players: TELE SANTANA, 51 on 26 July, took over the management of the team in April 1980. After choosing several goalkeepers he seems to have settled for VALDIR PERES (31) who was a reserve at both the 1974 and 1978 World Cups with PAULO SERGIO (24) as his reserve. LEANDRO (23) at right-back, the gifted JUNIOR (28 on 29 June) at left-back, in the middle of the defence OSCAR (28 on 20 June) and the new LUISINHO (23), with PERIVALDO (24), EDEVALDO (24), GETULIO (26) and JUNINHO (23) also in contention. The midfield is packed with players of the highest possible talent. BATISTA (27) appears to have totally recovered from an injury which had stopped him playing recently, TONINHO CEREZO (27) is an authoratative midfield player, and both SOCRATES (28) and ZICO (29) possess the right instincts in front of goal, but the real jewel in the crown might be PAULO ROBERTO FALCAO (28), who has spent the last two seasons playing for Roma in Italy. ROBERTO 'DINAMITE' (27) has returned after a spell in Spain and is scoring goals regularly, REINALDO (25), knees willing, is another forward whom Santana likes, and on the flanks there are TITA (24) or PAULO ISIDORIO (28) on the right, EDER (24) or MARIO SERGIO (31) on the left. Brazil will undoubtedly be among the favourites.

Russia

Football Federation founded 1912. Joined FIFA 1946.

Previous appearances: 1958 (Quarter-finalists), 1962 (Quarter-finalists), 1966 (Fourth) and 1970 (Quarter-finalists).

The present tournament: Headed European Group III with 14 points from 8 games. In front of CZECHOSLOVAKIA (won 2–0 at home and drew 1–1 away), WALES (drew 0–0 away and won 3–0 at home), ICELAND (won 2–1 away and 5–0 at home) and TURKEY (won 4–0 at home and 3–0 away).

The manager and players: KONSTATIN BESKOV, 61, was appointed in 1979 after Russia had failed to qualify for the 1980 European Nations championships and under his guidance Russia went through both 1980 and 1981 undefeated. RENAT DASSAEV (25 on 12 April) has been first-choice goalkeeper for the past two and a half years. TENGUIZ SULAKVELIDZE (25) is an authoritative right-back, ALEXANDR CHIVADZE (27 on 8 April) is a wonderfully gifted defender who is always keen to attack, SERGHEI BUROVSKI (26) is a tight central defender and SERGEI BALATCHA (24) is as gifted. Other defenders who have been selected recently have been JURIJ SUSLOPAROV (24), VAGIZ KHIDIATULLIN (23) and VLADIMIR LOZINSKI (26). That elegant playmaker DANIEL KIPIANI (30) should have recovered from a recent injury but other midfield players to have shone have been VITALY DARASEGLIA (24), SERGEI ANDREEV (26 on 16 May), HOREN OGANESYAN (26), LEONID BURJAK (20 on 10 July) and VLADIMIR BESSONOV (24). OLEG BLOKHIN (29) has recovered his sharpness in the attack, RAMAS SHENGHELIA (24) is another forward who has been scoring regularly and YURI GAVRILOV (25) has played several games in the centre, vying for the place with VLADIMIR GUTSAEV (29) team-mate to Shenghelia with Dinamo Tiblisi. BLOKHIN scored 6 times, SHENGHELIA 4 times in four matches, ANDREEV, OGANESIAN and GAVRILOV twice each.

Scotland

Scottish Football Association founded in 1873. Joined FIFA 1910–1920, 1924–1928, 1946.

Previous appearances: 1954, 1958, 1974 and 1978.

Present tournament: Headed European Group VI with 11 points from 8 games over NORTHERN IRELAND (drew 1–1 at home and 0–0 away), SWEDEN (won 1–0 away and 2–0 at home), PORTUGAL (drew 0–0 at home and lost 1–2 away) and ISRAEL (won 1–0 away and 3–1 at home).

The manager and players: Under the shrewd and experienced management of JOCK STEIN, who will be 60 in October, the team has been sensibly put together. ALAN ROUGH (29) has made the goalkeeping position his own but, apart from DANNY McGRAIN (32 on 1 May) at left-back, the defenders will all be experiencing their first World Cup: WILLIE MILLER (27 on 2 May) as stopper, ALAN HANSEN (25 on 13 June) as sweeper and FRANK GRAY (27) at left-back, with cover being provided by ALEX McLEISH (23), RAY STEWART (22) and ALLY DAWSON (24). The midfield has real skill, determination and flair with GORDON STRACHAN (25) a player of bite, GRAEME SOUNESS (29 on 6 May) one of the best playmakers in Europe and ASA HARTFORD (32) an experienced ball-winner. JOHN WARK (24) has a nice tendency to score goals and DAVID NAREY (26 on 6 May) has been in striking form this season. JOHN ROBERTSON (28) is a left-wing of real pace and trickery, JOE JORDAN (30) has had an unhappy season with A.C. Milan in Italy but is always a threat to defences, especially when the ball is in the air, ANDY GRAY (26) is a central striker of gifts and PAUL STURROCK (25) is an exciting recent discovery. But Scotland must hope that KENNY DALGLISH (31), one of the most gifted forwards in Europe, is fully on form and reproduces the dazzling qualities he has been displaying for his club side, Liverpool.

New Zealand

Football Association founded 1891. Joined FIFA 1948.

Previous appearances: None.

Present tournament: Qualified second behind KUWAIT in Asia–Oceania group. In their qualifying section New Zealand took 14 points out of 8 games against AUSTRALIA (drew 3–3 at home and 2–0 away), INDONESIA (won 2–0 away and 5–0 at home), TAIWAN (drew 0–0 away and won 2–0 at home) and FIJI (won 4–0 away and 13–0 at home: a record for the tournament). Then in the play-off finished Second with games against KUWAIT (lost 1–2 at home, drew 2–2 away), CHINA (drew 0–0 away and won 1–0 at home) and SAUDI ARABIA (drew 2–2 at home, won 5–0 away) and beat CHINA 2–1 in the deciding match in Singapore. 44 goals in 55 games.

The manager and players: That lengthy campaign of qualification has meant JOHN ADSHEAD (39) has managed to create a spirit of great camaraderie in his small squad. RICHARD WILSON (26 on 8 May) is first-choice goalkeeper with FRANK VAN HATTUM (24) as his closest rival. GLEN DODS (25 on 7 June), RICKY HERBERT (20) the stopper, ADRIAN ELRICK (32) the left-back and BOBBY ALMOND (30 on 16 April) the sweeper have as their deputies DAVE BRIGHT (29), JOHN HILL (32), GLEN ADAM (23 on 22 May) and SAM MALCOLMSON. The star of midfield is STEVE SUMNER (27 on 2 April), who scored six times in that 13–0 victory over Fiji, who is accompanied by ALLAN BOATH (24), DUNCAN COLE (24 on 12 July), KEITH MACKAY (25) and GRANT TURNER (23). Among the forwards will be WYNTON RUFER (19) who scored the decisive goal against China in the decider, STEVE WOODDIN (27), a tricky dribbler with a fierce left-foot shot, CLIVE CAMPBELL (27) and BRIAN TURNER (33).

7 SOME OF THE BEST PLAYERS ON VIEW

Giancarlo ANTOGNONI (Italy). Born 1 April 1954, he first played for Italy in December 1974 since when he has been a vital member of the team, making deep runs into attack from midfield. He had an unhappy time in the 1978 World Cup, being troubled by an ankle injury, and in November was badly injured in a League game playing for Fiorentina. One hopes that he will be completely recovered, for he could be one of the most exciting players on view.

Oswaldo ARDILES (Argentina). Born 3 August 1953, Ardiles was a member of the side that won the 1978 tournament and immediately after brought his talents, along with Ricardo Villa, to Tottenham Hotspur in England. He is a midfield player of great artistry, possessing pace, vision, an acute tactical sense and an enormous amount of energy.

Joao BATISTA Da Silva (Brazil) was born on 8 March 1955, played in all seven of Brazil's games in the 1978 tournament and is highly skilled at setting up attacks from deep in midfield.

Daniel BERTONI (Argentina). Born 14 March 1955, he is a fast and excitable winger who scored the last goal of the 1978 tournament before taking his talents to Seville in Spain. For the past two seasons he has been with Fiorentina in Italy, scoring goals regularly.

Roberto BETTEGA (Italy). Born 27 December 1950, he scored the goal which brought about Argentina's only defeat in 1978. A forward with a formidable technique, particularly in the air, he teamed up very well with Paolo Rossi and hopes to do so again.

Oleg BLOKHIN (Russia). Born 5 November 1952, Blokhin played in the 1972 Olympics and rapidly became a key player for his club side, Dinamo Kiev, as well as for the national team. European Footballer of the Year for 1975 (the last player to be elected from outside the West German Bundesliga), he is now in his best form since 1976, and recently gained the honour of scoring the most goals in Russian club football.

Rainer BONHOF (West Germany). Born 29 March 1952, he caught the public attention in the 1974 World Cup when he played magnificently in the West German midfield. He had a far less happy time in the 1978 World Cup but soon after moved to play for Valencia before returning home in June 1980. A ferocious taker of free-kicks, it was in Spain that he seemed to have rediscovered his former flair.

Zbigniew BONIEK (Poland). Born March 1956, Boniek had a marvellous tournament during the 1978 World Cup, and has won over 50 caps since making his first appearance on 24 March 1976. Talented and perceptive, Boniek is courted by several clubs in the West but has helped his present club, RTK Widzew Lodz, to gain recent championships in Poland.

Maxime BOSSIS (France). Born 26 June 1955, Bossis has gradually come to make the position of leftback his own. A hard winner of the ball, he played in two matches in the last World Cup.

Paul BREITNER (West Germany). Born 5 October 1951, Breitner played at left-back for the sides that won both the 1972 European Nations Championship and the 1974 World Cup before taking his talents to play for Real Madrid, where he was encouraged by Miljan Miljanic (the present manager of Yugoslavia) to move into midfield. There he is playing with much authority and is regularly scoring goals.

Hans-Peter BRIEGEL (West Germany). Born 11 October 1955, he used to be a decathlete as a junior. His first international was in October 1979 against France, since when he has become a vital member of the side, whether playing in defence or midfield.

Trevor BROOKING (England). Born 2 October 1948, Brooking is a player who has vision, technique and experience on the left side of the midfield and has won over 40 caps since first playing in April 1974. He should win his fiftieth cap in Spain.

Ivan BULJAN (Yugoslavia). Born 11 December 1949, Buljan played in the 1974 finals, subsequently took his talents as a defender to club football in West Germany and the United States, and should be a key member of the Yugoslavian side.

Leonid BURJAK (Russia). Born 10 July 1953, Burjak has long been a member of the Russian side as a defensive player in midfield, possessing a marvellous technique striking long passes to the attack.

Antonio Carlos CEREZO (Brazil). Born 21 April 1955, Toninho Cerezo played in the 1978 finals and is undoubtedly one of the most talented midfield players in the world; indeed critics have compared him with former stars such as Didi and Gerson.

Jan CEULEMANS (Belgium). Born 28 February 1957, Ceulemans is a strong and large-boned striker who possesses a fierce shot and who regularly scores goals.

Alexandr CHIVADZE (Russia). Born 8 April 1955, Chivadze is a cultured sweeper who possesses a fine counter-attack technique. Captain of the successful Dynamo Tblisi team, he won the first of his caps in 1980 and is now a valued member of this talented Soviet side.

Fulvio COLLOVATI (Italy). Born 9 May 1957, he is the only new addition to the Italian defence seen in 1978. An excellent stopper who scores regularly from set-pieces.

Bruno CONTI (Italy). Born 13 March 1955, he plays on the right side of the attack, having taken over the role of *tornante* so successfully fulfilled by Franco Causio.

Kenny DALGLISH (Scotland). Born 4 March 1951, Dalglish moved from Celtic to Liverpool in June 1977 and fitted in marvellously. The most-capped Scottish player, he is very difficult to mark and particularly dangerous when he has his back to goal, for he turns like a top. He also possesses a fierce left-foot shot.

Renat DASSAEV (Russia). Dassaev, who was born 12 April 1957, first played in September 1979 and has made the goalkeeping position his own. Brave and agile, he has quick reflexes and is in the line of great Russian keepers such as Lev Yashin.

Ramon DIAZ (Argentina). Born 29 August 1959, Diaz made his first appearance in 1979. A short, stocky player with a devastating right-foot shot he is a worthy teammate to Diego Maradona.

Marek DZUBIA (Poland). Born 19 December 1955, Dzubia is a constructive rightback who has made appearances in the midfield. He has played regularly since making his first appearance in April 1977 and this tournament should see his fiftieth appearance.

Paulo Roberto FALCAO (Brazil). Born 16 October 1953, he is the only Brazilian playing abroad likely to be used by Telé Santana. He has spent the last two seasons playing in Italy for Roma and possesses true class with his intelligence and vision as a play-maker in the midfield.

Elias FIGUEROA (Chile). Born on 25 October 1946, Figueroa played at centre-half in all Chile's games in the 1966 and 1974 World Cups. Now he plays a bit deeper, organising his defence, but will undoubtedly be one of the most skilful defenders on view in Spain. Was voted South American Footballer of the Year for 1974, 1975, and 1976.

Ubaldo FILLOL (Argentina). Born on 21 July 1950, Fillol played in one game during the 1974 finals before playing throughout the 1978 competition for the victorious Argentine side. Brave as well as experienced.

Trevor FRANCIS (England). Born 19 April 1954, Francis won his first cap in February 1977 and would have been an important member of the England side but for a cruel injury he received to an Achilles tendon in April 1980. Now fully recovered and playing with real skill for Manchester City, Spain should see him at his best; a sharp player with tremendous acceleration.

Claudio GENTILE (Italy). Born in Tripoli 27 September 1953, he was first
selected in April 1975 and has been one of the cornerstones of the Italian defence
ever since, whether playing at stopper or, as he does now, at right-back.

Eric GERETS (Belgium). Born 18 May 1954, Gerets began his career at centre-
forward but switched to the defence in 1973 and is now one of the best right-backs
in Europe.

Ivan GUDELJ (Yugoslavia). Born 8 November 1960, Gudelj is a defender who
has recently come into the national side and is very powerful when moving
forward.

Alan HANSEN (Scotland). Born 13 June 1957, Hansen moved to Liverpool
from Partick Thistle and has taken over as a left centre-back who can make
devastating incursions into the attack. He won his first cap in April 1979 against
Wales and is now a fixed member of Scotland's defence.

Glenn HODDLE (England). Born 27 October 1957, Hoddle is undoubtedly the
most gifted midfield player of his generation playing in England. If he comes
good in Spain he could lift the chances of England considerably with his accurate
passing, long and short, and his fierce shooting.

Pat JENNINGS (Northern Ireland). Born 12 June 1945, he will find it fifth time
lucky because he was first capped in April 1964 and has played in the qualifying
rounds of the previous four tournaments. A most respected goalkeeper, Jennings
has been one of the foremost in Europe during the past decade and is still on
magnificent form following the surprising transfer from Tottenham Hotspur to
Arsenal.

Leovegildo Lins Gama JUNIOR (Brazil). Born 29 June 1954, he is a most
effective leftback – harsh and quick in the tackle, able also to make devastating
runs into attack. Superb at freekicks.

Manny KALTZ (West Germany). Born 6 January 1953, Kaltz played unhappily
in the role of sweeper during the 1978 World Cup but now plays as a fast-moving
right-back who loves to attack. He scored five times in the qualifying competition.

Kevin KEEGAN (England). Born 14 February 1951, he was transferred from
Liverpool to Hamburg after helping the English side win the 1977 edition of the
European Cup, and is now back with Southampton. Elected European Footballer
of the Year for 1978 and 1979 he won his first cap in November 1972, but for the
past eight years has been an integral part of the English attack, making darting
runs into space, and has recently found his best form.

Mario KEMPES (Argentina). Born 14 July 1954, he has played in all of
Argentina's games during the 1974 and 1978 World Cups, and in the latter was
chief scorer with 6 goals. He spent four seasons playing with Valencia and was,
perhaps, the foremost player of the 1978 tournament although the only
Argentinian to be recalled and play.

Daniel KIPIANI (Russia). Born 18 December 1951, he is simply a princely
passer of the ball over all distances and has been a vital part of his country's plans
in the qualifying tournament. Sadly he broke a leg in the autumn, but will
thankfully be well enough to put his exciting skills on display in Spain.

Hans KRANKL (Austria). Born 13 February 1953, Krankl has returned to
Austria after having spent two unhappy seasons with Barcelona. He is scoring
goals again, however, and together with his team-mate Walter Schachner forms a
most penetrating spearhead for Austria, as well as having experience of Spanish
conditions.

LUISINHO (Brazil). Born as Luis Carlos Ferreira on 22 October 1958, he is a
central defender of great talent who is strong in the tackle and able to anticipate
trouble very skilfully.

Danny McGRAIN (Scotland). Born 1 May 1950, McGrain's career has been blighted by injury. The best fullback on view in the 1974 tournament he found himself being forced to miss the 1978 tournament and was out of the game for over a year. But he has returned to his top form and should be one of the best players on view in Spain.

Sammy McILROY (Northern Ireland). Born 2 August 1954, McIlroy teams up most effectively with Martin O'Neill in the midfield.

Diego MARADONA (Argentina). Born 31 October 1960, he was first selected to play on 28 February 1977 – eighteen months before the World Cup finals. It was a good thing that Menotti's team won the tournament without the infant prodigy because when Maradona has the ball he seems to possess all the gifts: breath-taking dribbling, exciting close control, a lethal shot. It's no wonder that he was elected South American Footballer of the Year on the past three occasions.

Marian MASNY (Czechoslovakia). Born 13 August 1950, he is a player of guiles and wiles on the right-hand side of the Czech attack. Plays a little deeper nowadays but is still very effective as a three-quarter.

Hansi MULLER (West Germany). Born 27 July 1957, he is a marvellously skilful player who possesses a natural left foot and is used to coming forward from midfield to score goals.

Zdenek NEHODA (Czechoslovakia). Born 9 May 1952, Nehoda was a crucial figure in the Czech triumph in the 1976 European Nations Championship and when the team gained third place four years later. He used to play on the left wing but nowadays brings his dribbling and shooting skills more into the centre.

Tibor NYILASI (Hungary). Born 18 January 1955, he is the true play-maker of the Hungarian side with his control, perceptive vision and ability to make telling runs into the attack. Tall and well-built, he is a formidable figure in the air.

Martin O'NEILL (Northern Ireland). Born 1 March 1952, he was first selected for a full international in March 1973 since when he has been a regular choice in midfield.

Jose OSCAR Bernardi (Brazil). Born 20 June 1954, Oscar played as central defender in all seven of Brazil's games in the 1978 World Cup. A well-built stopper, he still is mobile enough to make intelligent use of the ball after it has been won.

Antonin PANENKA (Czechoslovakia). Born 2 December 1948, Panenka is a glorious midfield schemer who did much to help win the 1976 European Nations Championship for his country.

Daniel PASSARELLA (Argentina). Born 25 May 1953, he was captain of the Argentine side that won the 1978 tournament. A highly intelligent player, he loves to make runs into the left side of midfield.

Vladimir PETROVIC (Yugoslavia). Born 1 July 1955, he is a midfield player of the greatest skill and vision, and played in the 1974 World Cup. Recently he has undergone several severe operations to his knees but when he is at his best form can be one of the most guileful play-makers in the world.

Bruno PEZZEY (Austria). Born 3 February 1955, he was transferred after the 1978 World Cup to play in West Germany. A tall, commanding centre-back, he first played for his country when he was twenty, is most effective when breaking forward at set-pieces, and often scores goals.

Michel PLATINI (France). Born 21 June 1955, Platini is the most gifted Player to have come out of France since Raymond Kopa in the Fifties. A real specialist with free-kicks he was first selected in March 1976, since when he has been a permanent fixture in midfield.

Herbert PROHASKA (Austria). Born 8 August 1955, Prohaska is a very gifted midfield player who appeared in the 1978 World Cup and has been with Internazionale of Milan for the past two seasons.

Bryan ROBSON (England). Born 11 January 1957, he is the only Englishman to have taken part in all eight games of the qualifying tournament. Robson can play in the defence or as a defensive midfielder and has the skill and the intelligence that come to all outstanding players.

Dominique ROCHETEAU (France). Born 14 January 1955, he played in the 1978 World Cup on the right wing, but now has brought his dribbling and shooting skills more into the centre. He was first selected on 3 September 1975, since when he is a fixed member of France's attack.

Paolo ROSSI (Italy). Born 23 September 1956, Rossi was first selected in December 1977 and became one of the key figures in the 1978 World Cup, linking up most effectively in the attack with Roberto Bettega. Adroit, with superb reflexes in the box, he has been banned from football for the past two years and all supporters of the Italian cause will hope that he can immediately recover his inspiring form.

Karl-Heinz RUMMENIGGE (West Germany). Born 25 September 1955, Rummenigge is an elegant winger who scores regularly. First selected in October 1976 he took part in the 1978 World Cup, was a regular member of the West German side that won the 1980 European Nations Championship and was elected European Footballer of the Year for 1980 and 1981.

Harald SCHUMACHER (West Germany). Born 6 March 1954, he came into the side for the 1980 European Championships after two of his rivals had been injured, and made the goalkeeping position his own. First selected on 26 May 1979, he has sure handling, positions himself well and distributes the ball intelligently.

Bernd SCHUSTER (West Germany). Born 22 December 1959, he was another influential figure in that West German victory with his fearless and skilful running in midfield. Soon after, he was transferred to Barcelona and although injured recently should have recovered in time for the World Cup.

Ramas SHENGHELIA (Russia). Born 15 October 1957, he has recently come into the attack as a winger who likes to cut in and score goals. Playing for the club side of Dynamo Tiblisi he is a team-mate of Chivadze, Darasegia Sulakvelidze and Kipiani.

Peter SHILTON (England). Born 18 September 1949, he won his first cap in November 1970, succeeded Gordon Banks after the latter was injured two years later in a road accident, and now shares the goalkeeping position with Ray Clemence, who is approximately a year older.

Didier SIX (France). Born 21 August 1954, he is a left-winger of real talent who scored two fine goals in the 1978 World Cup. A mercurial dribbler, he often finds himself criticised for being inconsistent.

SOCRATES Brasileiro Sampiode Viera de Oliciera (Brazil). Born 19 February 1954, Socrates is a tall attacking midfield player or striker who has been a regular member of the side for the past three years.

Graeme SOUNESS (Scotland). Born 6 May 1953, Souness is now displaying his skills as a midfield organiser with Liverpool whom he joined in January 1980. Selected for only one game during the 1978 World Cup, he has since come into the side on a regular basis and must be one of the most talented and inspired schemers in Europe.

Ulrich STIELKE (West Germany). Born 15 November 1954, he was transferred in 1977 from Borussia Moenchengladbach to Real Madrid, where he soon made his mark. A hard and skilful defender he should be a vital member of West

German plans.

Tenguiz SULAKVELIDZE (Russia). Born 8 December 1956, this cultured right-back was first selected on 26 March 1980 and has been a regular choice ever since. Plays for Dynamo Tiblisi alongside Chivadze.

Safet SUSIC (Yugoslavia). Born 13 April 1955, he has recently been out of the side doing national service. With a fine scoring record, he was first selected on 26 June 1977 against Brazil in Rio.

Marco TARDELLI (Italy). Born 8 September 1954, he was first selected at fullback in April 1976, but before the 1978 tournament was moved into midfield as a ball-winner, and has been a regular member of the team ever since. Tenacious, he is a very tight marker and a skilful distributor after the ball has been won.

Andras TOROSCIK (Hungary). Born 1 May 1955, he is the most gifted of forwards with superb ball-control, precise vision and a rasping right-foot shot. First selected in 1976, he played in the 1978 World Cup.

Marius TRESOR (France). Born in Guadaloupe on 15 January 1950, Tresor was first selected on 4 December 1971 as a central defender and was the only French player to travel through each minute of the three games in the 1978 World Cup, in which France used all her players.

Francois VAN DER ELST (Belgium). Born 1 December 1954, he is a forward of real skills who has played at right-half as well as right-back, and is now with West Ham United after passing time with New York Cosmos.

René VANDEREYCKEN (Belgium). Born 22 July 1953, he is an attacking midfield player of great flair, who has spent the last two seasons in Italy with Genoa.

Wilfred VAN MOER (Belgium). Born 1 March 1945, he took part in the 1970 World Cup and is a midfield playmaker of great guile.

Ladislav VIZEK (Czechoslovakia). Born 22 January 1955, Vizek was late in gaining selection but is a very tricky forward, particularly down the flanks.

Zlatko VUJOVIC (Yugoslavia). Born 26 August 1958, he is the twin-brother of Zoran who plays in the team's defence and was the top scorer for Yugoslavia in the qualifying rounds with 7 goals. A gifted right-winger, he won his first selection on 1 April 1979, and has been chosen ever since.

Kurt WELZL (Austria). Born 6 November 1954, he was recently transferred to Valencia for whom he has been scoring goals regularly.

Ray WILKINS (England). Born 14 September 1956, he was undoubtedly England's best player in the 1980 European Nations Championship but Ron Greenwood must be hoping that he has fully recovered from injury and is again able to take his place on the midfield.

ZICO (Brazil). Born as Artur Artunes Coimbra on 3 March 1953, Zico was first selected in 1975, since when he has been a regular member of the Brazilian attack. A player of great gifts, he experienced an unhappy time in the previous tournament but now is at his best and scored 5 times in the qualifying competition. Voted South American Footballer of the Year for 1977.

Wladyslaw ZMUDA (Poland). Born 6 June 1954, he will be playing in his third World Cup finals as a calm, thoughtful central defender who was first selected against Eire on 21 October 1973 and has been a regular choice ever since.

Dino ZOFF (Italy). Born on 28 February 1942 in the north-eastern part of Italy, he was first selected in April 1968, helped Italy win the European Nations championship of that year and played in both the World Cup finals of 1974 and 1978. His positional play is immaculate, his reflexes still sharp and he should make his hundredth appearance before the tournament commences.

8 SPAIN — THE RECORD, THE MANAGER, THE PLAYERS AND THE GROUNDS

In June 1980, José Emilio Santamaria took over as manager after he had been groomed to succeed Ladislao Kubala. Born in Montevideo on 31 July 1929 to Spanish parents, he played twenty-five games for Uruguay as a central defender before signing for Real Madrid, then the European Champions. With Real he went on to participate in four further Finals of the European Cup, gaining a Winners' Medal on three of those occasions, in addition to playing nine times for Spain. When his playing days were over he turned to coaching, first with the youth team of Real Madrid and later with the full side of Espanol of Barcelona. In September 1978 he was named as national coordinator of the Spanish side, working alongside Kubala.

Home advantage can be so important to the chances of a side. Playing in familiar grounds before thousands of enthusiastic supporters can really raise a team to new heights. Just examine the facts:

URUGUAY 1930 – Winners
ITALY 1934 – Winners
FRANCE 1938 – Beaten by eventual Winners
BRAZIL 1950 – Second
SWITZERLAND 1954 – Quarter-finalists
SWEDEN 1958 – Finalists
CHILE 1962 – Quarter-finalists
ENGLAND 1966 – Winners
MEXICO 1970 – Quarter-finalists
WEST GERMANY 1974 – Winners
ARGENTINA 1978 – Winners

In his period in office, Santamaria has attempted to accustom the International players of his country to the idea of playing more football by arranging matches for every month. In the June and July of 1981 he took his team on a tour which crossed over from Portugal to Mexico and finished in Brazil playing seven internationals against sides including Portugal, Mexico, Colombia, Chile and Brazil. The results weren't promising, but remember that in the year before the last World Cup

Argentina played a series of internationals against foreign opposition in which the primary aim was not to win at all costs but to meld together a group of the most talented players.

José Ramon ALESANCO. Born 19 May 1956, he is a powerful and athletic sweeper who marks very tightly and anticipates well. His skill in the air makes him an outstanding figure at corners or freekicks.

Miguel ALONSO. Born 1 February 1953, he has been brought into the midfield by Santamaria and has put on several outstanding displays.

Luis ARCONADA. Born 26 June 1954, Arconada is in the long line of outstanding Spanish goalkeepers. He possesses incredible reflexes and can be most effective when the ball is on the ground, but he can be indecisive when the ball is in the air.

José Antonio CAMACHO. Born 8 June 1955, Camacho was a left-back of some standing before a cruel injury robbed him of the opportunity of playing in the 1978 finals in Argentina. He has since made a full recovery and resumed his firm role in the defence.

'DANI' Born as Daniel Ruiz Bazan on 28 June 1951, Dani is a small, slight player of skill who likes to come in from the wing to score goals.

ESTEBAN VIGO BENITEZ. Born 17 January 1955, he made his debut last September and showed himself to be an elusive left-wing.

Rafael GORDILLO. Born 4 February 1956, he plays on the left side of the defence and likes to move forward. He played most effectively in the 1980 European Nations Championship finals.

JOAQUIN Alonso. Born on 9 June 1956, he is a tall, well-built player who operates on the right side of the midfield where he makes telling use of his strength in defence.

'JUANITO'. Born as Juan Gomez on 10 November 1954, he is a forward of the most exciting gifts and temperament: sharp, with superb ball-control, he seems to spot openings in a defence seconds faster than other players. He can be his own worst enemy, however, as he tends to lose his cool.

Roberto LOPEZ UFARTE. Born 19 April 1958, he made his debut in September 1977, then disappeared from view and has only recently won his place back in the side as a skilful left-winger.

Antonio MACEDA. Born 26 May 1957, he made his debut against England in March 1981 and had an outstanding match in the middle of the defence, anticipating quickly and using the ball well.

MARCOS Alonso. Another who made his first appearance in that match, Marcos, who was born 1 October 1959, is a young forward of great promise and usually plays on the left wing.

Enrique Castro 'QUINI'. Born 23 September 1949, he has for several seasons scored many goals in club football in Spain. His name was in the news during March 1981 when he was kidnapped.

'SANTILLANA'. Born as Carlos Alonso on 23 August 1952, he vies for the role of central striker with 'Quini' and Satrustegui. A team-mate of 'Juanito's', he has stupendous skill in the air.

Jesus SATRUSTEGUI. Born 12 February 1954, he leads the attack of Spain with verve and aggression, laying off balls well to those at his side and scoring frequently himself.

Enrique SAURA. Born 2 August 1954, he usually plays wide on either wing.

Miguel TENDILLO. Born 1 February 1961, Tendillo has moved in from playing on the right hand of the defence to becoming a stopper. He first played in June 1980 and has since been a regular member of the defence.

VICTOR Munoz. Born 15 March 1957, he is a defensive midfield player who covers every blade of grass with his aggressive running.

Jesus Maria ZAMORA. Born 1 January 1955, he really came to the fore in the 1980 European Nations Championship when he played three outstanding matches. A real force in midfield, he can suggest play with either his passing or forceful running and will undoubtedly be one of the major lights of these Finals. He was sadly off-form on that summer tour last year and it showed.

The Grounds for the 82 World Cup

Group 1 :   VIGO (BALAIDOS) 56,790
             CORUNA (RIAZOR)34,190

Group 2 :   GIJON (EL MOLINON) 45,153
             OVIEDO (CARLOS TARTIERE) 28,421

Group 3 :   ALICANTE (ESTADIO JOSE RICO PEREZ)
             35,886
             ELCHE (NUEVO ESADIO) 53,290

Group 4 :   BILBAO (SAN MAMES) 46,223
             VALLADOLID (NUEVO ESTADIO) 29,990

Group 5 :   VALENCIA (LUIS CASANOVA) 47,542
             ZARAGOZA (LA ROMAREDA) 41,806

Group 6 :   MALAGA (LA ROSALEDA) 34,411
             SEVILLE (BENITO VILLAMARIN) 50,253

Second Round matches at :

BARCELONA (NOU CAMP) 125,000 which also stages the
opening match
BARCELONA (SARRIA/ESPANOL) 40,400
MADRID (BERNABEU) 90,800
MADRID (MANZARES/CALDRON) 65,695

Semi-final at :

BARCELONA (NOU CAMP) 125,000 and SEVILLE
(SANCHO PIZJUAN) 68,110

THIRD PLACE play-off :

ALICANTE (ESTADIO JOSE RICO PEREZ) 35,886

Final : MADRID (BERNABEU) 90,800

9 COMPLETE FIRST ROUND DRAW

GROUP ONE

June 14	Italy	Poland	(Vigo, 5.15)
June 15	Peru	Cameroon	(Coruna, 5.15)
June 18	Italy	Peru	(Vigo, 5.15)
June 19	Poland	Cameroon	(Coruna, 5.15)
June 22	Peru	Poland	(Coruna, 5.15)
June 23	Italy	Cameroon	(Vigo, 5.15)

GROUP TWO

June 16	West Germany	Algeria	(Gijon, 5.15)
June 17	Chile	Austria	(Oviedo, 5.15)
June 20	West Germany	Chile	(Gijon, 5.15)
June 21	Algeria	Austria	(Oviedo, 5.15)
June 24	Algeria	Chile	(Oviedo, 5.15)
June 25	West Germany	Austria	(Gijon, 5.15)

GROUP THREE

June 13	Argentina	Belgium	(Barcelona, 8.00)
June 15	Hungary	El Salvador	(Elche, 9.00)
June 18	Argentina	Hungary	(Alicante, 9.00)
June 19	Belgium	El Salvador	(Elche, 9.00)
June 22	Belgium	Hungary	(Elche, 9.00)
June 23	Argentina	El Salvador	(Alicante, 9.00)

GROUP FOUR

June 16	England	France	(Bilbao, 5.15)
June 17	Czechoslovakia	Kuwait	(Valladolid, 5.15)
June 20	England	Czechoslovakia	(Bilbao, 5.15)
June 21	France	Kuwait	(Valladolid, 5.15)
June 24	France	Czechoslovakia	(Valladolid, 5.15)
June 25	England	Kuwait	(Bilbao, 5.15)

GROUP FIVE

June 16 Spain	Honduras	(Valencia, 9.00)
June 17 Yugoslavia	N. Ireland	(Zaragoza, 9.00)
June 20 Spain	Yugoslavia	(Valencia, 9.00)
June 21 Honduras	N. Ireland	(Zaragoza, 9.00)
June 24 Honduras	Yugoslavia	(Zaragoza, 9.00)
June 25 Spain	N. Ireland	(Valencia, 9.00)

GROUP SIX

June 14 Brazil	Soviet Union	(Seville, 9.00)
June 15 Scotland	New Zealand	(Malaga, 9.00)
June 18 Brazil	Scotland	(Seville, 9.00)
June 19 Soviet Union	New Zealand	(Malaga, 9.00)
June 22 Soviet Union	Scotland	(Malaga, 9.00)
June 23 Brazil	New Zealand	(Seville, 9.00)

Who plays whom after the first round

Second round (June 28 to July 5)

Group A: Group one winners, group three winners, group six runners-up (Barcelona, Nou Camp)
Group B: Group two winners, group four winners, group five runners-up (Madrid, Bernabeu)
Group C: Group six winners, group one runners-up, group three runners-up (Barcelona Sarria)
Group D: Group five winners, group two runners-up, group four runners-up (Madrid, Calderon)

Semi-final round (July 8)

Winners of group A v Winners of group C (Barcelona, Nou Camp)
Winners of group B v Winners of group D (Seville)

Third place play-off (July 10)

Semi-final round losers (Alicante)

FINAL (July 11)

Semi-final round winners (Madrid, Bernabeu)

GROUP 1	GROUP 2	GROUP 3
ITALY ✶ POLAND PERU CAMEROON	W.GERMANY ✶ ALGERIA CHILE AUSTRIA	ARGENTINA ✶ BELGIUM HUNGARY EL SALVADOR
GROUP 4	GROUP 5	GROUP 6
ENGLAND ✶ FRANCE CZECHOSLOVAKIA KUWAIT	SPAIN ✶ HONDURAS YUGOSLAVIA N.IRELAND	BRAZIL ✶ USSR SCOTLAND NEW ZEALAND
✶ Denotes Top Seeds		